The ART of
INSIGHT

OTHER BOOKS BY CHARLES KIEFER

*Action Trumps Everything: Creating What You Want
in an Uncertain World*
with Leonard A. Schlesinger and Paul B. Brown

*Just Start: Take Action, Embrace Uncertainty,
Create the Future*
with Leonard A. Schlesinger and Paul B. Brown

The ART of
INSIGHT

HOW TO HAVE
MORE AHA! MOMENTS

Charles Kiefer · *Malcolm Constable*

Berrett–Koehler Publishers, Inc.
San Francisco
a BK Life book

Berrett-Koehler Publishers, Inc.
235 Montgomery Street, Suite 650
San Francisco, CA 94104-2916
Tel: (415) 288-0260   Fax: (415) 362-2512   www.bkconnection.com

Ordering Information
Quantity sales. Special discounts are available on quantity purchases by corporations, associations, and others. For details, contact the "Special Sales Department" at the Berrett-Koehler address above.
Individual sales. Berrett-Koehler publications are available through most bookstores. They can also be ordered directly from Berrett-Koehler: Tel: (800) 929-2929; Fax: (802) 864-7626; www.bkconnection.com
Orders for college textbook/course adoption use. Please contact Berrett-Koehler: Tel: (800) 929-2929; Fax: (802) 864-7626.
Orders by U.S. trade bookstores and wholesalers. Please contact Ingram Publisher Services: Tel: (800) 509-4887; Fax: (800) 838-1149; E-mail: customer.service@ ingrampublisherservices.com; or visit www.ingrampublisherservices.com/Ordering for details about electronic ordering.

Berrett-Koehler and the BK logo are registered trademarks of Berrett-Koehler Publishers, Inc.

Printed in the United States of America

Berrett-Koehler books are printed on long-lasting acid-free paper. When it is available, we choose paper that has been manufactured by environmentally responsible processes. These may include using trees grown in sustainable forests, incorporating recycled paper, minimizing chlorine in bleaching, or recycling the energy produced at the paper mill.

Library of Congress Cataloging-in-Publication Data
Kiefer, Charles F.
The art of insight : how to have more aha! moments / Charles Kiefer and Malcolm Constable. — First edition.
     pages cm
Includes bibliographical references and index.
ISBN 978-1-60994-809-2 (pbk.)
1. Insight. 2. Problem solving. 3. Thought and thinking.
I. Constable, Malcolm. II. Title.
BF449.5.K54 2013
153.4'3—dc23   2012051813

FIRST EDITION
17 16 15 14 13   10 9 8 7 6 5 4 3 2 1

Cover design by Steve Pisano
Book design and production by Beverly Butterfield, Girl of the West Productions
Copyediting by PeopleSpeak
Indexing by Rachel Rice

Contents

Introduction:
Aha Moments

One insight can change your life, and the next can change your organization, or even the world.

We are all born with the capacity for insight, a capacity that remains with us our entire lives. Insights are those "aha" moments when the clouds part and the solution to your problem arises right in front of you. They happen when fresh new light is spread on a subject you've considered for some time. With insight, we enjoy wisdom, balance, and perspective. We have all experienced these moments of deep understanding, even if we might not know what to call them or how to describe them. They occur while we're showering, jogging, daydreaming, sleeping, or talking with someone about unrelated subjects. Suddenly, usually when we are not consciously thinking about the subject, an answer pops into our heads. The fog lifts. The issue is clarified. The confusion dissolves. And the situation becomes so simple and so obvious that we can't imagine how we missed it before. Surprisingly, these moments can be made to occur with much greater regularity. With them, you will find new paths of thought and new solutions that are permanent and easy to implement.

Think of a tricky problem that you have lived with for too long in either your work or your personal life. No doubt, you have had insights toward solving this problem. You experienced new thoughts on the subject that provoked a deeper understanding. Or you saw something fresh that lifted your spirits and washed away a low mood, clearing the space for a new line of inquiry. As we explore the nature of insight, you'll see how these past experiences can help you reconnect with the principles and source of your insights.

Our goal is for you to generate insights quickly and easily.

Our goal is for you to generate insights quickly and easily so that with greater regularity, you can access them when you need them most.

Put simply, if you want more insights in your life, this book is for you. It is a concise guide to simple actions that can help anybody cultivate a habit of having more frequent and timely insights. With the appearance of more insights, you will make better decisions, find solutions to difficult problems, and offer fresh thinking on any subject.

Regrettably, for most of us, life trains us out of employing this natural thinking process, and we lose the habit of making insight a more regular and expedient occurrence. The approach and methods offered in this book will reconnect you with that ability and help you increase the frequency, strength, and value of the insights you experience each day.

If you feel like you make poor decisions, getting stuck in ruts of low-quality thinking; if you continually feel the need to work hard to overcome resistance; if you would like to experience more confidence, more resilience, and a greater sense of peace; or if you simply want more insights, both big and small, in your life, then this book is for you.

Based on what people who have mastered the methods in this book report, you should experience the following benefits at work and at home:

- Your problems won't hang around and will often seem to solve themselves.

- You'll make decisions more quickly, with greater confidence, fewer mistakes, and better overall judgment.

- Your interactions with other people will improve.

- Your personal schedule will relax, and you will find time to live and work with ease.

- Energy will be freed for the things you care about.

- Meetings will be shorter and flow efficiently.

- Better decisions will be made.

- Solutions will emerge that are easily implemented.

All these phenomena are a result of an improved capacity for insight.

The applications for what we have termed The Art of Insight (TAOI) are limitless. Whether you want to make better decisions, solve intractable problems, understand others better, or gain a new perspective on anything, insights are the answer.

> The applications for what we have termed The Art of Insight (TAOI) are limitless.

3

As you read further into this book, you are going to appreciate something that you have always suspected, if not known. There is no set recipe for how to have more insights. And, unlike the formulaic steps in many business and self-improvement books, the practice of Insight Thinking is more art than science. Insight is a form of thought, and of course, everyone thinks a bit differently, just as everyone paints or writes differently. Like any art, it can be developed. With practice and attention, we can foster this innate capacity and enjoy the many benefits of a more insightful life.

This Book

We're going to give you a summary of what's in this book. First, we want to call your attention to the difference between what we term *intellectual learning* and *insight learning*. We hope you'll read and absorb this book with the latter.

Intellectual learning relies on accumulating facts, processing those facts, storing those facts in memory, and then connecting them in a very methodical and thoughtful way. Insight learning works differently: it's active in the sense that we are looking for insights, but it also occurs passively on its own through a subconscious reflective process that is more receptive than active. Often very diverse facts we already know are put together in a new way. Insight learning is all about *seeing something for yourself* and not just storing new information in your memory bank.

Both of these types of learning are very valuable, but while you are reading this book, we hope you will aim for insight learning.

The Book in a Few Pages

We believe there are two reasons you are not having as many insights as you could. First, you may not realize you should be looking for insight. Our thinking is aimed mostly at interrogating our memory for solutions to problems. The operative assumption is that the answer lies in memory if we could only access it. But as you will soon see (and probably know already), an insight is a thought we've *never* had before. It's a *fresh thought*. If you want an insight, you don't want to replow what you already know yet another time; you want to look into the unknown. This is common sense: if you know what you are looking for, you are more apt to find it. So chapter 1 is aimed at helping you clarify what insights are for you. After you do so, we promise they will be easier to find.

Second, while the circumstances in which people have their insights are as varied as the individuals, everyone we have talked with has reported a common *state of mind*. It's an easygoing, unpressured, open, and ungripped state. The more often you reside in this state of mind, the more often you will have insights. Conversely, when you are agitated and bearing down with your thinking, insights become more elusive. While the Insight State of Mind is our natural, default state, we inadvertently think ourselves out of it. We simply need to regain our natural capacity to gravitate toward a good state of mind in order to have more insights, as outlined in chapter 2.

For all we know, insights are available all the time, but we just aren't hearing them. Maybe our thinking radio is tuned to a different channel; maybe our mental grinding acts like a nearby construction site, drowning out the insight channel entirely. The remedy is learn to *listen for insight*, and this is the focus of chapter 3.

We have found that while you can take many of the actions we suggest in this book and consequently have more insights in your life, you run the risk of signing up for a lifetime of *unnecessary* work. In chapter 4 you will see that being insightful is a function of how you think, and as you daily deepen your appreciation and understanding of how thought works for you—having insight into your thinking—you will discover that insights will be brought to you in the course of life with no work on your part whatsoever.

Here are the four key elements of The Art of Insight:

- Understanding what insights are and actively looking for them

- Occupying a state of mind in which you're apt to have insights more frequently

- Learning how to listen in such a way that you hear insights in yourself and others

- Growing your understanding of how thought works in your life

In chapter 5 we offer practical illustrations of TAOI being used by individuals, and then in chapter 6 we illustrate how it is used in organizations.

The accounts in this book should be used to stimulate your own insights. Reflect on what resonates and strikes true for you. Even when you don't relate to something, it can still help you sharpen your own understanding. Remember, a state of mind cannot be expressed fully with words. Our language can only point you in the right direction.

Where This Book Came From

Over the course of our combined forty years of management consulting, we became increasingly fascinated by the observation that so many intelligent executives, although armed with pages upon pages of data, logic, and analysis, nonetheless ended up making boneheaded decisions. It wasn't a rare occurrence. And yet we saw exceptions. From time to time, clients on their own accord, or sometimes with our help, achieved a strategic insight—a simplifying aha moment that often radically redefined their business and the competitive space to their advantage. Once articulated, these strategic insights seemed like simple common sense to everyone. They were easily understood and acted upon. In fact, implementation usually occurred with far less effort than the forced march that often characterized strategy implementation.

Could that phenomenon become a more regular occurrence? Was there some sort of formula for it? How might we go about looking for it?

For more than fifteen years we have helped senior managers realize that the phenomenon of insight itself holds the key to these questions. As we explored these concepts with our clients, we found that it is indeed possible to increase the frequency, strength, and traction of insights, and by doing so, improve both thinking and decision making.

In the course of our explorations, we reviewed research on the subject, but what we found to be far more useful were the numerous conversations we had with professionals engaged in helping executives, managers, and their teams be more insightful. When given a few basic principles and methods, clients reported having more insights and exhibiting better judgment as a matter of course. They solved problems more quickly and identified and avoided potential mistakes with greater regularity. Moreover, the plans and strategies they developed were creative and enduring—significant departures from prevailing thought and straightforward and unfettered in their implementation. As you might expect, what we learned about insight is far more widely applicable than just for improving business performance. All the principles we've found apply equally well to the activities of daily living.

Imagine what it would be like to live a more insightful life. Through our shared experiences and with stories from our clients, colleagues, and friends, we hope you will join us on a quiet walk through our discoveries about practical insight, learning how you can increase the frequency and quality of your insights every day.

How to Read This Book

We would like to encourage you to read this book in a slightly different manner than you might be used to. Below you will find some tips about how you can approach reading so that you can absorb the concepts in a deeper way than you might otherwise. In addition, we hope you will take advantage of the Online Learning Experience that accompanies this book on our website TAOI Online Learning (see the link in "Online Learning Experience" in the back of the book).

Developing Insight Is an Art and an Empirical Science

Earlier we observed that everyone has the innate capacity for insight. Developing it is an art, and in this field, everyone is an artist—latently, a very capable one. But like any art, it requires practice to develop fully.

Insight is a topic that has yet to be scientifically pinned down. We have great respect for the scientific method, and in this conversation, we are going to point toward empirical science as contrasted with theoretical science. Everything we posit should be and is testable in your everyday situations. So, you need not believe the concepts as you read them. In fact, it's better if you don't believe. Instead, simply allow yourself to make your own discoveries about insight and about how you think. Then, test your findings to see if they work for *you*. Use your own life as a laboratory. Here is an illustration.

Thirty years ago, Charlie read a transcript of a keynote speech by Willis Harman, professor emeritus of engineering at Stanford University and then-president of the Institute of Noetic Sciences. Willis spent the latter part of his career working on how to study consciousness scientifically. Addressing intuition, Willis observed that if we have an intelligence within us that is greater than rational thought alone, then it is reasonable to allow that intelligence to inform *all* our daily choices and actions. Charlie remembers the experience of reading that speech:

I can't recall Willis's exact words, but they triggered a thought for me, and I resolved to test my realization with my own personal experiment. For the next twenty-four hours, as best I could, I based every action on my intuitive sense of what was right—unless a rational assessment showed it to be ill-advised. Instead of prioritizing activities, as I had been taught in time-management classes, and mechanically marching through my design of the day, I selected my first task on the basis of what intuitively felt right and continued this method as I completed each task. (I did make all my scheduled meetings, calls, and so forth, on time.) I remember being faced with a couple of choices of minor consequence. I made them on the basis of feeling and without analysis. Someone (I can't recall if it was a member of my staff or a client) came to me with a proposed course of action, along with a sound argument in favor, but it didn't feel right. We had a conversation, and a better alternative surfaced.

The outcome? I had a simply fabulous day! It was clear I should continue the experiment, in no small part to rule out any possibility of a fluke. The following day was equally terrific! I extended the experiment until the end of the week, and in a sense, I'm still going. Over the years, I haven't replaced rational thought, but my intuition developed as a legitimate and often-employed complement to reason. Typically, I revel in a thorough analysis and explore all known alternatives, crunching the numbers on a

spreadsheet—I can go on quite a tear. Then, I switch
off the intellect entirely and check in with what I feel
and what my intuition tells me.

While insight isn't exactly the same as intuition, we've in-
cluded this story here to illustrate the value of running disciplined experiments. We hope you will try this sort of testing
and self-assessment as you read this book.

Interest within the scientific community in insight, intuition, cognitive science, and the nature of thought has grown
considerably in recent years. A great deal of research has been
conducted, and much has been written on topics such as neuro-
psychology, neurophysiology, and consciousness. By contrast,
the source material for this book is based on our experience
and on the experiences of our clients. While the findings we
share are generally consistent with the formal research we have
come across, we have decided to focus on practical approaches
that you can apply to your community, workplace, and life.

What You "Hear" When You Read Is More Important Than What We Write

In the course of our explorations of insight, we attended many
meetings and lectures on the subject. Charlie recalls how during
one of these lectures, George Pransky, a prominent psycho-
therapist, spoke about insight, psychological well-being, and
related ideas:

> I listened quietly, as George instructed us, letting his
> words float through my head without thinking too
> much about them. Suddenly, a rush of energy hit me,

and I had a flash of awareness—a new understanding of how the reality we experience is formed by our thoughts. Moments later, I had a second flash. A major part of my prior understanding was completely reversed! The simplicity of these realizations was, for me, awesome; issues that had intrigued me for thirty years now made sense in a new way.

After George's speech, I approached him, grateful and excited. "My God, George, that was great! I've been pondering these things for years. Now it's all clear to me: why things work the way they do, why life turns out the way it does." I repeated back to him what he had said, and George responded with the shy, sheepish grin I've come to know well: "I'm so pleased for you, but I don't think I said any of that. In fact, I don't think I was even talking about the things you now say you just discovered."

Taken aback, I thought, "What's going on here?" I somehow misunderstood what he was saying, yet I had had a life-changing insight. A few days later, I had still another realization: when it comes to insights, what *you hear* is more important than what *someone else says*.

Remember What You Already Know

Here's something that you will find really comforting: if you want more insights in your life, you don't need to learn much more. All of us already hold all the knowledge and experience that we need.

Samuel Johnson is said to have observed that people need to be *reminded* more often than they need to be *instructed*. Most authors have a new idea they want you to learn, but since you already know all you need to about insight, simply explaining our ideas or those of our clients and colleagues won't suffice. Nor will extolling the value of insights—you already know this as well. What we *will* try to do is show you how to have *more* insights. Of course, we don't know how you think, so teaching you how to think differently could be quite a challenge. Luckily for you and us, we don't have to tackle this. Instead, we will focus on helping you find and reclaim that which you already know.

Think of this book as a conversation guiding you toward where to look for insight, not just advice on the specifics of what to do. Very little of our conversation may strike you as new, but fortunately, this means you have nothing to memorize. Even better, anything you rediscover automatically becomes more present in your life—with no further work on your part whatsoever.

As you read, don't be concerned with remembering facts or grasping the material with your intellect. Instead, let yourself capture the topics intuitively. Look for as many insights as you can. Later, we will examine why a bit of latitude or imprecision in language and analysis can help you find more insights. Once you experience an insight of some sort, ask yourself, "Does this really make sense?" Try it out over a few days. Just *notice* whether it's true. Don't worry about doing anything with it. Ultimately, everything true should be observable in some way.

By immersing yourself in our stories and examples of the principles of insight, you will begin to habitually access your

best thinking—to the point where insight and wisdom will occur with greater frequency in your life. However, our experience has shown us that the principles are not a "prescription"
to be followed. Rather, the key is for you to look for your own
insights about these principles. A few stories can't prove a
point, at least not a scientific point. Our examples show how
you can find your way back to a nice, easygoing state of mind
where fresh thoughts can occur.

An artist, Carolyn, once had a teacher who talked constantly during class about art, technique, and anything else that
came to his mind while his students were painting. During the
first few days of class, Carolyn found Michael's chatter distracting, but she didn't say anything since it was apparently his style
and no one else seemed to have a problem with it. As time went
on, she learned to tune out the prattle and immerse herself
more deeply into her painting. One day, she explained (with a
sense of pleasure) how the chattering had actually trained her
to become more deeply immersed in her painting. It helped
her attain an effortless focus where she was less conscious of
the chatter of her internal mind. As she spoke to us about this,
she had an insight: this must have been Michael's intent all
along—jabbering away to get his students "out of their heads"
and into their art. Let our stories about insight serve the same
function for you.

Reading This Book for Insight

Psychologists have identified a state of mind that is most conducive to insights. Although more than a few of our clients say
they get insights while reading, only a small percentage report

reading as their *primary* path to insight. Those who get insights while reading generally describe being in a quiet place, deeply engrossed in a subject, as opposed to skimming pages or rushing through an e-mail. Insights that occur during reading are often not about a concept the writer is addressing. Instead, they are often new understandings about something indirectly related, like Charlie experienced while listening to George Pransky. Sometimes, the insights are entirely unrelated.

Nevertheless, reading can be a very powerful tool. In 1977, reading an article by the management consultant Dave Berlew provided one of the most important insights of Charlie's professional career. In the article, Berlew described the power of what he termed Common Vision—an idea he and others employed in the Peace Corps—and the extraordinary results it produced. Connecting Berlew's ideas to his own understanding of the relationship between thought and reality, Charlie saw why Common Vision worked and founded Innovation Associates based on that insight.

How does one read for insight? We haven't discovered a universal answer, but we bet you have an answer that works for you. Pause for a moment and think of a time when you had an insight while reading. What was the setting? For the most part, you probably find it less effective to cram your reading into tiny slots during the middle of a crowded day. It's better to clear a block of time and allow for reflection as you read. What helps you get the most out of your reading? How would you be most apt to absorb something of significance? Consider our exploration of insight an invitation to know yourself more deeply.

You may notice that you like to do your reflective reading before you go to bed, when the time seems ripe to read contemplatively. You'll meet our colleague Ed later. His wife calls this *gazebo reading*, a time when she can let everything disappear for a while.

Online Learning Experience

Reading about insight is one thing. Acting on what you read is quite another. This book is supplemented with web-based exercises and illustrations that are an important complement to this text. We have developed these exercises over the past fifteen years, and if you use them, you will connect with and absorb the methods in this book in a deeper and more permanent way. In any art, practice is all-important.

Finally, when we began our exploration for methods to increase insight and wisdom, one of our early challenges was that none of our clients had any sense of how often they currently had insights; they only knew that insights didn't come as frequently as they would like. We wanted to teach our clients some of the ideas we were discovering, but in the absence of a baseline, how could we clearly discern whether someone's "insight meter" had actually changed? In the section titled "Assessing Your Progress," you will find an exercise to gauge how your capacity for insight is changing. If you are interested in this, you may want to jump to it to create a baseline before you read much further.

If you put the insights and methods of this book to good use, you will become a more effective thinker. Fresh ideas will abound. You will make better decisions quickly and confidently. You will find solutions to long-standing problems. And you will ultimately enjoy a more effortless and engaging life.

The path to finding insights is simple, but simple things are sometimes not so easy. If you sharpen your image of what an insight is and reconnect with the clearheaded, calm, and receptive state of mind you dwell in when insight occurs, rest assured, you will have more insights. We aim to provide you with guidance and practical steps to increase the frequency, strength, and quality of the insights you experience each day. You will learn how to cultivate your own Insight State of Mind and practice Insight Listening while having more insights on the topics that matter to you most.

1 What Is Insight?

If you know what you're looking for, you're more apt to find it. That's as true for finding insights as it is for tracking down a lost pair of socks.

Knowing that you want more insights gives clear direction for your unconscious mind to go to work and find an answer. The clearer you are about the specific insight you seek, the more regularly the insight will occur. It's just like when you are considering buying a new car and you suddenly notice more cars on the road like the one you want to buy. Pause for a moment to pick a problem or topic you'd like some insight into and set it aside for use in the coming chapters.

Let's begin with how insight differs from other types of thought. While what follows is what we have learned from others, what an insight means for us or them is not nearly as important as what an insight is *for you*. With this awareness in place, you can learn how to actively listen for insights and access the state of mind in which you are most apt to facilitate insights.

Insights Are Thoughts

Insights are a specific type of thought. We may think we understand what thoughts are, but let's take a closer look anyway. For our purposes, we are going to adopt a loose definition. Thoughts are ideas, opinions, mental images, cognitive activities, or any internal activities of the mind.

Thoughts ebb and flow naturally all the time. If you were asked to think about an orange balloon, that image would appear in your mind for a moment, and then it would vanish.

Sometimes we create our thoughts by actively looking for them. The most common example of this is in problem solving. When our first thoughts don't yield a solution, we try to bring forth new thoughts. In some cases, thoughts appear unsolicited, and we simply notice their arrival.

We are not consciously aware of many types of thinking. For example, when driving a car, we may suddenly notice that we had been absorbed in thought and were not conscious of our driving. Of course, while our minds wandered at the wheel, we continued to have many subconscious thoughts telling us to slow down, accelerate, or bear right. Although rarely vocalized and never visible, these thoughts exist and are essential for driving. It is important to remember that while we may be aware of some thoughts, a great many more are constantly occurring without our noticing.

Memory Thoughts Versus Fresh Thoughts

Thoughts are constantly occurring, even when we are asleep. We have already had most of the thoughts that occur to us in some form or another. We call these *memory thoughts*. Memory thoughts often occur not just once or twice but many times, like a social security number or an ATM code. *Fresh thoughts*, on the other hand, are new thoughts that we have never had before. Fresh thoughts are new for you even if they are old for someone else.

The distinction between a fresh thought and a memory thought is useful when exploring the nature of insight. Insights are always fresh thoughts, but not all fresh thoughts are insights. You might say to yourself, "Wow, look at that flower" or "This dinner is one of the best in my life." These are fresh thoughts, but we would not describe them as insights. And just because a thought or idea is fresh does not necessarily mean it is good. Fresh or not, any thought that proves wrong would not be termed an insight. In fact, fresh thoughts are frequently way off base. Nothing's wrong with having fresh ideas that are useless, as long as they serve as part of your creative process and you don't necessarily act on them.

Most of the answers we need every day lie in memory, and there is no reason to look for an insight if the solution is already known. If the solution is not known, then memory thoughts are no longer sufficient, and fresh thoughts become essential. Memory thinking seems to have a self-reinforcing nature. With each use, we learn to depend

> Insights are always fresh thoughts, but not all fresh thoughts are insights.

more and more on it to solve our problems to the point that a strong reliance is established. Our educational institutions reinforce this pattern by stressing the accumulation of facts and the application of logical reasoning and generally encouraging us to become proficient memory thinkers. Thus, when faced with a question, our minds look first, and often exclusively, to our memories. When we get stuck in memory-based thinking, we are unconsciously disconnecting ourselves from our natural capacity for insight.

Fresh thoughts have a distinct, albeit often-unnoticed, feeling associated with them. A light, spacious sense of surprise or even joy accompanies a fresh thought. The presence of such a feeling can alert you that something novel has arrived. Even ideas that turn out to be poor can appear with a good feeling at the outset. Of course, some fresh thoughts carry an ugly feeling, like wanting revenge and suddenly seeing a new way to get it. Even though they are fresh, these hopefully rare cases would not be called insights.

To Have More Insights, Have More Fresh Thoughts

Trying deliberately to have an insight in any given moment rarely works, as we will see in upcoming chapters. What you can and should do is be deliberate about having more fresh thoughts. You have to discipline yourself to look for something fresh. Sometimes your fresh thoughts will be good, and other times they will be bad. You can learn to discard the bad ones, and over time the increase in fresh thoughts will yield an increase in insights.

You Need Both Kinds of Thoughts

Of course, you don't have to create everything completely from scratch. Memory, knowledge, and the thoughts that accompany them are essential. And you must grasp the basic fundamentals of what you are doing. For example, a lawyer needs a strong understanding of case law, but the best attorneys are not those who just remember the most from law school. They also have the ability to come up with an original and persuasive approach to a case. The best doctors are knowledgeable about pathology and human physiology, but they are also skilled at applying that knowledge insightfully to a particular medical case or condition.

In the case of insight, we operate more effectively when memory thoughts are present in the background and fresh thoughts are out in front, but the right relationship between fresh and memory thoughts is not just about having one kind in the back and one kind in the front of the mind. A healthy interplay between the two must be active and ongoing. As your memory bank grows and expands, you accumulate more raw material for insights. If you are trying to become well versed in a subject, you must search for more information and more ideas outside your own and add them to your memory bank. Nobel laureate Linus Pauling believed memory of isolated facts lay at the core of creativity. Pauling's Caltech students were reported to complain bitterly at having to memorize facts they could easily look up. One of his students, Dr. Samuel E. George, paraphrased Professor Pauling's response:

> It's what you have in your memory bank—what you can recall instantly—that's important. If you have to look it up, it's worthless for creative thinking.

> [Pauling] proceeded to give an example. In the mid-1930s, he was riding a train from London to Oxford. To pass the time, he came across an article in the journal *Nature*, arguing that proteins were amorphous

globs whose 3D structure could never be deduced. He instantly saw the fallacy in the argument—because of one isolated stray fact in his memory bank—the key chemical bond in the protein backbone did not freely rotate....

He began doodling, and by the time he reached Oxford, he had discovered the alpha helix [for which he later won the Nobel Prize in Chemistry].[1]

Insights Deepen Understanding

All insights are fresh thoughts, but as we said before, only a few fresh thoughts turn out to be insights. So what distinguishes an insight from a fresh thought? The short answer is the quality of the thought. Insights are really high-quality fresh thoughts. They result in a dramatically improved understanding of a situation or problem such that we see things more deeply and more accurately than before.

In some cases, we have no prior understanding of the subject in question whatsoever, while in others, our understanding (seen from the postinsight perspective) is either limited or wrong. The bigger the difference between the new understanding and the old, the more dramatic the insight will seem to be.

Imagine for a moment that for some time you have been troubled by someone's behavior. You can't understand why he does the things he does. One evening, you are watching someone on public television explain how people's minds work. You comprehend what the speaker is saying, and if you were asked to take a test on the subject, you would pass based on your intellectual understanding. Although the subject is interesting, it does not feel particularly relevant to you at the moment.

Suddenly, your experience is a flash of clarity. You see the big picture and you absorb abruptly and instinctively, in a personal and even visceral way, what that person on television was talking about. All the speaker's logic and facts fall into place, and you see how everything works together. In this same instant, you realize why the person who has been troubling you behaves the way that he does. You feel a combination of surprise, satisfaction, pleasure, and relief.

In this example (which could be about something completely different—from a scientific theory to a new way to keep leaves out of your gutters), two separate things are occurring. The first is a realization and the second is an insight. When you discover or realize something, you understand it at face value, such as when you finally comprehend what someone is trying to explain to you *in the way she intends you to understand.* Discoveries and realizations are typically characterized by the appearance of new mental maps where none existed before, and like insights, they can be accompanied by an aha experience.

Insight is a discovery or realization that goes beyond face value, beyond the obvious. It is a deeper, more universal understanding.

Insight is a discovery or realization that goes *beyond face value,* beyond the obvious. It is a deeper, more universal understanding that is often very relevant to you.

Insight is often characterized by the upending of an existing concept. The difference between a discovery or realization and an insight is not a sharp line, nor does it need to be for our purposes. The more realizations and discoveries you experience, the more likely it is that you will have an insight.

While most thoughts that occur during arguments are taken personally, when a true insight arrives, the situation or problem becomes more clear and *less* personal. The insight broadens the point of discussion, takes it in a new direction, or dissolves the conflict altogether.

Don't forget the important distinction between intellectual understanding and insight. Insight includes an intellectual understanding but goes further with a deeper awareness. With insight, a new cognitive structure is formed that is different from the sum of its parts, and it usually calls for a different action. In other words, action A might have been appropriate at first, but after the insight, action B is clearly the better course.

Insights Make Things Simple and Maybe Even Fine the Way They Are

Before we understand anything completely, we perceive it as complex. As soon as we understand the situation and the insight arrives, we wonder how we could not have seen it before. The new understanding connects existing elements in our thinking, rearranging what we know; the pieces were already in place—just not in the right place. Understanding connects the pieces and makes your understanding of reality more accurate. Sometimes our new understanding is universal, like the elegance and beauty scientists speak of when they arrive at a more fundamental appreciation of a phenomenon.

Often insights reveal that a situation we once deemed a serious issue is in fact not a problem at all—that things are actually fine the way they are. Or it may turn out that the issue is unchangeable, and the insight brings the realization that this is not such a bad thing and that there is something to be done in the face of that immutability. In these cases, insights dissolve the fear, frustration, and anxiety attached to the issue. They restore our equanimity and help us see the problem in a new light, providing new perspectives and new opportunities.

A few years back, Charlie and our colleague Robin Charbit were sharing their ideas about insight with the management team of a large organization. Over the past few years, this particular business unit had failed repeatedly to introduce new products into their marketplace, which was not only frustrating but a source of real fear for the management team. Charlie and Robin gave a brief overview of The Art of Insight and then proposed that the team spend an hour using the ideas to explore their problem.

About half an hour into their discussion, an insight hit: *every other company in their industry was having even more difficulty than they were on exactly the same issue.* Then another insight came shortly after that: the characteristics of the industry had so changed that simply rolling out new versions of existing products was no longer the path to success *for anyone.* The room filled with an enormous psychological sigh of relief. Immediately, the team discarded the track they had been on and devoted the remainder of their discussion to applying their resources into distinctly different areas. You can imagine the amount of money they saved by abandoning this dead-end course!

Insights Result in Changed Perception

Following an insight, we see the world differently. Sometimes the difference is only slight, and other times it can be quite profound. One common experience where insights prove useful is struggling with the behavior of a friend or relative, particularly when we find ourselves chronically feeling defensive or angry. One day you may learn something about the person's history and realize why he is prone to behave a certain way. In that one instant, the negative feelings dissolve, often to be replaced by a sense of connection, empathy, and compassion.

One colleague, whom we will call Joan, describes hating her sister for fifteen years. It got to the point that not only did she not want to be around her, but when the sister's name came up in conversation, even in reference to someone completely different, Joan would tighten up. One day, while talking with a friend about her difficult upbringing, Joan realized her sister had created a unique way of insulating herself from their trying family situation. Although Joan and her friend weren't talking about the sister, the sister's behavior suddenly made sense. Joan knew she didn't want to live in the "alternative universe" her sister had created for herself, but she knew now why it existed—and all her negative feelings simply evaporated.

Joan's story about seeing her sister in a new light illustrates how in the moment of clarity that accompanies insight, compassion can transform anger and fear into understanding, appreciation, and even love. As with the case of Joan and her sister, insights into another person are particularly powerful because not only do they change your view of that person going forward, but they are capable of rewriting the entire history of your relationship to the point that previously hard-to-swallow experiences and memories disappear entirely.

From the moment we are struck by an insight, what once looked natural and right may suddenly appear foreign and wrong. Lifelong smokers, even after years of accumulating reasons to stop, acquiring all the medical justification, and failing to break the habit time and time again, may simply toss out their last pack of cigarettes, never to pick it up again after experiencing an insight. In the wake of an insight, acting in new ways is easy and takes less energy than when we try to move our thinking in a new direction by force of will alone. Willpower alone is sustainable for only so long. Ultimately, it gives out.

Having an Insight Is Not Necessarily the Same as Solving a Problem

While one of the most common applications for insight is in solving a problem, it is not necessary to reach an impasse before looking for an insight. Insights unrelated to specific problems happen all the time. It is common to have insights on topics we are simply curious about. While having an insight and solving a problem are related, they are not one and the same. You can have insights when you don't have a problem, and you can also solve problems without insight. Some problems can be answered using logic and facts already stored in our minds, but for others, an insight is essential.

Insights Are Sometimes Nonverbal

Insights are sometimes too deep to express in words. In the wake of an insight, you may get excited and want to share the experience with others, but have you ever tried to explain your new insight to a friend, only to have her look at you and say, "So what? What's new about that? You've known that for years!" Other friends may feel your excitement but not have the slightest idea what you're talking about and respond in a similarly disappointing and uncomprehending manner.

Our friend Eliot Daley attended one of our Insight Thinking workshops a year ago. He was in the middle of writing his fourth book. Early in his career, Eliot had spent three years as president of Fred Rogers's production company, where he wrote all the scripts for *Mister Rogers' Neighborhood* and was acknowledged by critics and peers as a gifted writer. After *Mister Rogers,* Eliot wrote thousands of pages of reports that changed the directions of companies and published op-ed pieces and other journal articles. He was both talented and prolific. Even his e-mails were small literary delights. One morning Eliot had an insight in our workshop.

Here is a quote from Eliot's fifth book, *Formerly Called "Retirement,"* which he wrote from start to finish in two weeks in the wake of his insight. The passage describes a process in which Eliot and two partners were in a staged conversation during our workshop, having received the following instruction: "You have exactly one minute to share the issue or question you want an insight on. Then you must listen silently to the conversation of your two partners."

When it was my turn, I posed my question. . . . And they began considering my brief, blunt query. Of their seven minutes of dialogue together, I heard only one thing—ten seconds' worth. The young financier drew his right index finger across the left side of his chest as he quietly observed, "It sounds as if Eliot hasn't decided what he wants on his name tag."

My God! Oh, my God! An insight flared in my head like a sunburst, fierce and hot, searing itself into my mind: I have to decide! This isn't something that just happens to me. I have to decide!

I never thought of that before. I've been waiting, but nothing was happening. I was going nuts, and on the verge of getting depressed, but still nothing changed. It never, ever dawned on me that it was just as simple as deciding on my identity. This is not a matter of fate—this is a free choice: Who do I choose to be?

Well, who do I choose to be?

A writer.

The answer was instantaneous, unequivocal, certain. A writer. The answer leapt up from forever in my life. A writer. That is who I am, and that is who I choose to be. That is my identity, from this instant onward and ever.

Oh, my God! Everything in the universe became clear in that moment. If I am a writer—not an unemployed jack of all trades who also "does some writing" or "is working on a book," but a writer—then I just need to start acting like a writer, living like a writer, being a writer.

It was all so clear. The difference between what I do, and who I am. If I am a writer, then that will determine what I do, not the other way around. If I am a writer, then I organize my life, shape my priorities, spend my time, protect my space the way a writer would.

Now a robust agenda of transformational actions bloomed in my mind. Being that I am a writer, I need to create a proper space for writing. That means purging what had become my "office" of everything that dilutes or contaminates its new role as my "studio." No more a dumping ground for whatever matters might claim my attention. No more a cluttered jumble of distracting and distressing diversions from what matters in my life. No more anything but a serene environment dedicated to delivering whatever was within me. I'd find new space in the house to transform into a "home office" and cart over there everything not related to my writing. From now on, I would never use my studio for anything but writing. Fait accompli. Sure, I hadn't yet stirred from the conference room to actually take any of these actions, but they were as good as done. And I knew it.[2]

Reading the complete narrative of Eliot's insight is well worth your time. We share this story because Eliot bubbled with enthusiasm about his insight, telling all his friends he was a writer, but we already knew that! Eliot was the best writer we knew. Even though we could clearly tell something very important had happened to him, for us, Eliot's insight wasn't an insight at all; it was just the obvious and simple truth.

To some degree, every insight takes you into a way of knowing what lies in the unknown, before conscious thought, in a territory that cannot be expressed in words. This inability to express a personal insight in words may indicate its importance. Often, the more important the new understanding, the harder it is to explain. This was certainly true for the life-altering insight Charlie had, which for thirty years he tried unsuccessfully to describe to others in hope of finding someone who could really grasp and thus share his experience. Finally, he approached theosophist Sydney Banks, whose insights formed the basis of Dr. George Pransky's work.

> I briefly related the incident and asked him if he knew what it had meant. Syd replied with something like, "Well, it was a really important experience for you." I told him I knew that, but what did it mean? He replied again, "Well, I can tell it was a really important experience for you." That was it? I was extremely disappointed. Once again I had been unable to share this experience, and I remained bothered for a couple of months—until one day another insight hit. Maybe that's all it was: an important experience *for me*. Despite how life altering my insight was, it carried no great obligation of profound meaning to anyone else. All that mattered was that it meant a lot to me.

Insights Are Both Natural and Common

We think of insights as being quite rare, but smaller ones occur all the time and are often unnoticed. Discovering a new simile to explain something to a child, figuring out why your teenager did the most incomprehensible thing, finding a new path to work, or locating your keys when your spouse placed them in a never-before-used spot—all of these can be thought of as miniature insights. By noticing these tiny, everyday realizations—in essence, catching yourself doing something right—you become increasingly receptive to larger insights.

If you observe one- to two-year-old children, you'll notice that they seem to have realizations constantly. We have had clients tell us that they find themselves having insights while hanging out as their children play on the floor with blocks and crayons. This puts the clients in a nice state of mind, so they find themselves having fresh thoughts and insights right there on the carpet.

If the biggest reason we don't have insights is because we aren't looking for them, the second biggest is that we are not used to *listening* for them. We'll address this further in chapter 3. With the volume setting for most insights positioned between "moderate" and "quiet," an active mind filled with memory thinking will often drown them out, just as ambient noise can drown out a softly playing radio. When we are not engaged in listening to the loud music of memory thinking, we open ourselves to the opportunity to hear the fresh idea that may have been there all along. If an insight is not loud enough to be heard when it first appears, the potential for hearing it will persist as long as the problem stays with you. You need only seize the opportunity. Although it may not be provable, our working premise is that we are never given a problem without a solution. An insight is available to every problem if we can but hear it.

You may have had the experience of driving past a shop several times only to realize on the fourth pass that that store sells the spare part you have needed for several weeks. For some reason, the first three times you drove by the store, the thought didn't come to mind even though the shop was there, as was your need for the part. You simply missed the message. In the movie *August Rush*, the title character is a child prodigy who, speaking of the music he hears in his mind, asks his mentor, "Only some of us can hear it?" His mentor replies, "Only some of us are listening."[3]

Here is an example of an insight Charlie had while discussing TAOI with a friend:

> One of my most interesting recent insights was not verbal but rather manifested itself as a feeling. I was discussing TAOI with my friend, who chairs a university psychology department and is an authority on pain management. He commented, as do many, on the connection between the occurrence of insight and a state of relaxation, so essential to pain management. He noted that one of the most reliable and easily learned methods of achieving a relaxed state is to slow one's respiration rate to five breaths per

minute or less. The average person breathes twelve to fifteen times a minute or more.

He went on to ask me a suspiciously simple question: "How many parts are there to a breath?" As you might imagine, I answered, "Two." He pointed out that a breath can consist of three parts: inhalation, exhalation, and relaxation. He remarked that almost everybody misses the third part. Beyond being conceptually sound, this insight somehow soaked deeply into my body. Since then, I have found myself lying in bed most mornings, breathing in, breathing out, and resting until I feel a natural urge to take the next breath in. With my respiration rate well under two breaths a minute, waking up is one of my most fertile times for insights, and I have learned it is for many others as well.

As important as this process has been for my overall well-being, the ramifications have gone far beyond what I would have expected. I now see that deliberate relaxation is often overlooked as a fundamental element of being effective. After this discussion with my friend, I started advising my clients (executives who, like me, are used to pressing ahead 100 percent of the time) to relax the pressure, rest, and watch what happens before moving forward again. Not only have I noticed that I take my own advice with this approach more often, but I think my new understanding has worked its way into how I naturally experience the world in general.

When a fresh thought hits, we gain a new understanding no matter how small the subject matter. Sometimes an insight will occur and it will carry with it all the characteristics of an insight, but it will lack conscious understanding. Something will have changed, but you can't quite put words to what it is. Other times you might have a new thought that carries the good feeling of an insight even though it doesn't connect to anything specific in that moment. Only later do you link the thought to some subject of interest, as is the case when you have an insight while reading a professional journal and then months or even years later put that new understanding to work.

The key is to look for fresh thoughts. Look into the unknown, not just into your memory banks. Be mindful of your fresh thoughts, invite them in, and be sensitive to their occurrence, and they will increase in both frequency and quality. Remember that despite the value of both insight and problem solving, having an insight is not always the same as solving a problem. If you only ask yourself for an answer to a problem, habit and the way you have been taught to think may unconsciously limit your search to your memory. On the other hand, if you look toward having an insight, your unconscious mind will find creative solutions in both your memory and the unknown.

2 The Insight State of Mind

Now that you have a good fix on what insights are, let's move on to making ourselves receptive to their occurrence. Insights occur in a variety of circumstances. People report that insights are most likely to happen when they are walking or running, showering or meditating, playing with children, conversing with friends, watching a movie, listening to music, sleeping, golfing, or daydreaming. The list is perhaps as varied as the number of individuals.

While circumstances and settings for insights vary greatly, the one characteristic that they all share is a state of mind. All of us seem to recognize this easygoing "Insight State of Mind" in which our thinking is at its best. The mind is relaxed and not pressing in or fixating on a problem. Our attention is softly focused and may even be on something else entirely. Insights also occur when we are deep in logic and data analysis, but even then it's generally when we are experiencing a bit of reverie. Like when you're looking at a Magic Eye image, the picture appears one way until you relax your focus and allow a different image, the hidden and sought-after one that was there all along, to reveal itself.

Here is the second key to having more insights: insights, wisdom, and good judgment come from a clearheaded and calm state of mind. The way to have more insights is to spend more time in this receptive state. As you come to better recognize *your* Insight State of Mind, you will know when and how to look for it, and you will find yourself in this state more frequently, even in instances when you don't need an insight.

> Insights, wisdom, and good judgment come from a clearheaded, calm, and focused state of mind.

Consider thought as operating on a continuum. At one end of the spectrum, your thinking is structured, deliberate, and personal. You work hard to push it, managing its direction. You feel as if there is no separation between you and your thoughts because, in that state, you are your thoughts. You are in your head and in control. At the opposite end, your thinking just happens with no urgency or impulse to act. Thoughts occur, but with most of these, you are just a passive observer, watching whatever shows up. Here, thoughts have their own trajectory and lives of their own, but to varying degrees you can guide them, like when you daydream or when your mind wanders just before sleep. In these moments, you are present, but it doesn't feel as though you are entirely running the show. If you take one step further, you become lost in a dream, with no control over your thinking whatsoever. *Presence* is a good word to describe this end of the continuum; it is a state where very little active thinking takes place.

If you are like us, you aren't truly aware in real time of where your thoughts stand along this insight/intentionality continuum. When we address business issues, we try to use two distinct modes that correspond roughly to each end of the continuum. In the first, the trick is to think hard, listing all the relevant material and mentally arranging the pieces. Next, we follow these relationships to logical conclusions and then keep track of which logical paths hold water and which don't. Is this mode familiar to you? Like a sieve of logic, when it works, the best solution falls out. In the second mode, we drop all active thinking and, either figuratively or actually, gaze into the distance as we wait for whatever forms in our mind. We deliberately forestall any active connection making and see what springs forth on its own. Sometimes, as in a dream, the issue shifts of its own accord and offers a new perspective. Other times, it will feel as though we are groping in the unknown, a train of questions replacing a train of logic. This mode may sound familiar to you as well.

You will not be surprised to learn that insights often occur when you are not actively thinking about the problem at hand. Instead, insights arise when you are involved in something other than solving the problem, particularly something enjoyable or light on the mind. How often do you forget someone's name only to have it pop back into your head after you change the subject or shift mental gears? Between the two extremes of this continuum are many other modes, none inherently better than another. Think of putting on a pair of ice skates and sliding into the most appropriate mode for each moment rather than getting stuck in any one particular place. Sliding effortlessly from mode to mode is what we do when we are at our mental best. We move into one self to prepare our tax forms and slide into a different self to love our families. We instinctively place attention on what matters most, depending on what is required in the moment. We can focus our intellect for a few minutes, back off to a daydream, dive into memory for a short while, and then return to being present again. We are most naturally effective, most comfortable, and most productive when we enjoy a resilient state of mind.

Tempo and Pause

As a general rule, the Insight State of Mind feels slower and less hurried than your normal pace of thinking. In our earliest understanding of the insight process, we advised our clients to slow their thinking down. We found this was not a good prescription, however, because we are all quite different thinkers. Some people have insights as life zooms along, in which case slowing down could interfere with their process. Other people need the mental space of slower-paced thinking. Whether thought rips along at the speed of light or creeps at the pace of a snail, insights more often than not come during moments of mental pause.

The *art* of insight asks that you let the pace of your thinking settle into what is right for the moment. This takes personal awareness and practice. Just as there is no strict rule or formula for how fast you should play a certain piece of music, there is no prescription for the right tempo of thought. What is critical for facilitating insight is thinking that is neither rushed nor pressured.

A friend recently returned to playing classical piano with a certain amount of discipline:

> To my surprise, I discovered that with some effort and a little practice, I could play more than one of the preludes and fugues in Bach's *The Well-Tempered Clavier*. As most pianists can attest, *Clavier* is an amazing set of works, in part because many of the pieces we normally play quickly also sound beautiful when played more slowly. If I slowed down and practiced enough, I could play some of these magnificent studies, despite my limited abilities. Of course, I get into trouble and make plenty of mistakes when I try to play too quickly, but on the other hand, the pieces don't sound right when I play too slowly. My challenge is to find the right tempo for my mood and my skill. When I find it, I make music. When I don't, it's something else. In the words of Goldilocks, "This one's too hot, and this one's too cold, but this one is just right."

Our friend and colleague Steve uses a sports analogy for finding the Goldilocks sweet spot: "It is the championship game. Your team has the basketball with fifteen seconds left on the clock, and you are down by a point. Do you want to be wound up and tight or loose and confident?"

Great players always want the ball in these situations, and they are always loose and confident—present in the situation, open to whatever happens, and able to integrate many hours of practice into the immediate unfolding of the game. Lesser players get tight and try too hard to find the "right" action to take. Their breathing gets labored, and neither their brains nor their muscles move with the fluidity necessary to make the shot. They get so locked up that we use the term *choke* to characterize their efforts.

Bill Russell, star center for basketball's legendary Boston Celtics, describes a quiet mind in a very fast setting:

> Every so often, a Celtics game would heat up so that it became more than a physical, or even a mental, game and would be magical. That feeling is very difficult to describe, and I certainly never talked about it when I was playing. When it happened, I could feel my play rise to a new level. It came rarely, and would last anywhere from five minutes to a whole quarter or more. Three or four plays were not enough to get it going. It would surround not only me and the other Celtics, but also the players on the other team, even the referees.
>
> At that special level, all sorts of odd things happened. The game would be in a white heat of competition, and yet somehow I wouldn't feel competitive—which is a miracle in itself. I'd be putting out the maximum effort, straining, coughing up parts of my lungs as we ran, and yet I never felt the pain. The game would move so quickly that every fake, cut, and pass would be surprising—and yet nothing could surprise me. It was almost as if we were playing in slow motion.
>
> During those spells, I could almost sense how the next play would develop and where the next shot

would be taken. Even before the other team brought the ball into bounds, I could feel it so keenly that I'd want to shout to my teammates, "It's coming there!"—except that I knew everything would change if I did.

My premonitions would be consistently correct, and I always felt then that I not only knew all of the Celtics by heart, but also all the opposing players, and that they all knew me. There have been many times in my career when I felt moved or joyful, but these were the moments when I had chills pulsing up and down my spine.

Sometimes the feeling would last all the way to the end of the game, and when that happened, I never cared who won. I can honestly say that those few times were the only ones when I did not care. I don't mean that I was a good sport about it—that I'd played my best and had nothing to be ashamed of. On the five or ten occasions when the game ended at that special level, I literally did not care who won. If we lost, I'd still be free and high as a sky hawk.[1]

Obviously, a quiet mind does not necessarily mean that *you* are quiet. You might be mentally quiet but also very physically active, like Bill Russell operating in the zone. You may have your best insights when you're in the middle of a rapid discussion or friendly argument. We use the term *friendly* because insights rarely occur when the parties are feeling angry, afraid, or insulted.

The Space Where Fresh Thoughts Appear

Think of your mind for a moment as a conveyor belt filled with cafeteria trays going to the cleanup station. Each tray is a different thought moving along at a comfortable pace. Thoughts come in and go out, each flowing easily into the next, without pressure or urgency. Between each tray is a sense of space, a breath, or a pause living between each thought. This empty space is where fresh thoughts and insights occur.

Trays run faster on some belts than on others, but there is usually a constant flow, at least until the trays get stuck and begin to pile up on each other. With real cafeteria trays, you get a heap of dishes and a sticky, gooey mess. With thought, you become bothered, anxious, or overfocused. Your thoughts are now a jumbled traffic jam, piling up on one another. The space between thoughts, the nothingness where fresh ideas have the potential to pop up, has been crowded out. Less space leaves less room for insight. If you feel pressured, anxious, concerned, or worried, an insight is probably not on the horizon.

When an answer doesn't occur to us right away, we often get uncomfortable with this emptiness. We fill these gaps with thoughts from our memory bank, destroying the mental silence that could have brought us something fresh. As we shed this vexation and learn to be at ease with the unknown, we increase exponentially the likelihood of experiencing an insight.

One of our client teams was hammering away at a thorny problem without much success. Switching over their production line from one product to the next was taking too long. So, what could be done about it? Their mental cafeteria trays were pretty well piled up. We suggested that they begin looking for gaps, deliberately trying to relax their thinking and to practice not thinking about the problem—or about anything, for that matter. The room got pretty silent for a few minutes. Then one team member voiced a fresh thought that instantly crystallized into an understanding of how to adapt an existing component from a different line. With the addition of this component, they would be able to switch over in a matter of minutes instead of nearly an hour. Minding the gaps allowed this client team to create space in their thinking and see the problem differently.

Notice your own state of mind right now. Is your mind quiet and settled? Is there space between your thoughts, or are they crowding each other? Are you rushing through your reading, trying to get to the end as quickly as possible? Just noticing the quality of your thinking in this moment will help you recover an easygoing mental state. As soon as you stop thinking your way out of it, your natural equanimity will return.

Having read all this, you might think you have to do a lot to get your thinking into the right tempo, but you don't. It's much simpler than that. You just have to look for the good feeling of your Insight State of Mind, and as we will see in the next section, the pace of your thought will take care of itself.

The Feeling of the Insight State of Mind

The most reliable way to recognize the Insight State of Mind is by the presence of its characteristically good feeling.

There is a sense of calm, ease, and peace about it. There is a blue sky, a sense of spaciousness and that all is right with the world. While similar to the flow state that athletes like Bill Russell and performing artists speak of, the Insight State of Mind does not necessarily involve the peak experience often associated with being "in the zone." The Insight State of Mind feels more akin to a gentle walk home along a familiar route: peaceful and unlabored. A related but different good feeling accompanies the arrival of an insight. It carries a sudden sense of energy and elation. Think about how great it feels when a problem you have stewed over dissolves in a flash of insight. Whenever an event in your experience matches a new cognitive structure in your mind, the physiological response is usually a smile.

The feeling of the Insight State of Mind is subtle. You may notice it before an insight hits, but usually it reveals itself in the satisfaction you experience after the immediate excitement has passed. You'll observe it once the situation has settled down and your thinking feels more sharp and lucid. When you are both present in and appreciative of the moment, the feeling of an Insight State of Mind will be evident. Other types of good feelings, like that of completing a task or finishing a long run, while joyful, are not quite what we mean by the feeling associated with an Insight State of Mind.

The more familiar you become with this feeling, the more you will be drawn to finding it. As you find it more frequently, you will spend more time in the Insight State of Mind, and by spending more time in this state, you will become more insightful. Orienting yourself toward experiencing this good feeling is the most important touchstone in your insight practice.

Like reading a barometer, reflecting on this feeling gives you a moment-by-moment report on the quality of your thinking. The presence of such a feeling signals a good state of mind. It means that you are connected to your inner wisdom and that you have positioned yourself well to have an insight. When this feeling is absent—when you feel cloudy, confused, pressured, or angry—having an insight is less likely. Cultivating your awareness of this feeling takes you simultaneously to the feeling and to the Insight State of Mind. It's that simple. While you may not find it easy to do at first and the challenge may require some mindfulness, over time it will come naturally and more frequently.

Orienting yourself toward experiencing the good feeling of the Insight State of Mind is the most important touchstone in your insight practice.

The key is to have the sensor (the feeling) hooked up to the meter (your awareness) and to have the operator (you) paying attention to what the meter reads. Many of us, particularly men, may not spend much time in a mode where we notice our feelings. Instead, we retreat into our thoughts and find ourselves oriented toward figuring things out. In handling many matters, this may be the most useful mode of operation, but when an Insight State of Mind is required, we must remember to check in with our inner barometer.

It's like sending an invitation to your friends to come over for dinner. Instead of going out and rounding each of them up to bring to your home, you know that if you put out the invitation, eventually your friends will arrive. You don't need to spend any more energy than that. You do, however, need to stay alert for their arrival. Obviously, you don't want to miss them when the doorbell rings.

A beautiful day, a sail on an open sea, the perfect ski run, the moment you wake up in the morning, the recovery after your morning jog, the peace after meditation or prayer: life abounds with examples of relative mental peace. We use many words to try to describe the condition, and while none quite capture the essence, they can point toward it. For any deep feeling, descriptions through words are only pieces of the truth, but remember what these moments are like and you'll be heading in the right direction.

Losing and Recovering the Insight State of Mind

It will come as no surprise that during a normal workday, most of us don't spend much time in the Insight State of Mind. Circumstances like multitasking, meeting deadlines, and participating in conference calls all conspire against a good state of mind and lower the quality of our thinking. We are forever slipping unconsciously into worry, disappointment, fear, and other forms of insecure thinking. Since all these disruptions form ultimately from thought, you would think that we should be able to notice them and change our minds, but unfortunately, we get stuck and don't notice the moods that we fall into because the quality of our thinking is so off. In these moments, our thinking becomes dense, and a bad feeling sweeps through us to boot.

Unfortunately, there are many ways to enter these under-productive states: overusing of the analytical mind, not getting enough sleep, facing a poor performance review, dealing with a lost sale, encountering an angry colleague, making changes in diet, or dealing with physical ailments. Since physical and emotional stressors all cause us to get derailed, each of us has multiple routes to disaster. What may trigger one of us may have no effect whatsoever on another. Even when not triggered, our latent thinking habits can kick in and make us worry or be overly critical, which can draw us out of good spirits and make matters far worse. Since we are generally unaware that these storms of thought are occurring, we usually just press on. More often than not, the more we press, the more our state of mind deteriorates. We end up less creative, more inclined to make mistakes, and less conscious of our mental state.

A good first step is to become better at recognizing when you are not in a good state of mind. When you've lost the good feeling, you probably will not know the best thing to do in the moment. With just a small pause, however, you can remember that, at the very least, you should not be making any important decisions. Instead, wait until your mood has recovered. Sometimes, your waiting period is quite short, but occasionally you may need a good night's rest.

> Understanding the relationship between thought and experience makes weathering any bad mood easier.

Still, noticing the absence of a good feeling and stopping whatever you were doing changes your experience only if it

precipitates a change in thinking. Understanding the relationship between thought and experience makes weathering any
bad mood easier. While it may not work 100 percent of the
time, consciously looking for pleasant feelings can often interrupt the grip of a low mood and allow your mind to return to
a calmer, quieter state.

Our colleague Robin realizes that anything he attempts in
these situations, including trying to recover his mood, is likely
to be flawed. Who among us hasn't decided to stay at work an
extra thirty minutes to clear our e-mail in-box? We often hate
the decision as soon as we have made it, and the next day we
may find that many of the reply messages we had sent are of
questionable quality. In a case like this, our poor thinking may
result in twice as much new work as was necessary in the first
place. What's going on here? The extra thirty minutes in themselves don't cause the poor-quality work. Resentment degrades
our judgment and carries a very negative feeling.

Now, Robin has become better at stopping everything the
moment he discovers he's not in a good state of mind. He
simply waits until his mind settles. With a little practice and
patience, he needs only a couple of minutes to recover enough
common sense to know what to do next.

When we try to escape a bad mood, our strategies for doing
so are the products of low-quality thinking and therefore are
rarely successful. Many clever methods like replacing negative
thoughts with positive thoughts or initiating distractions have
been devised to change thinking. Unfortunately, trying to use
the mind to outfox the mind is never-ending work. The good
news is that all that effort is unnecessary. We come equipped

at birth with a simple barometer for high-quality thought: the presence or absence of the good feeling.

You might think that recognizing a bad state of mind is some sort of panacea for improving your state of mind, but it isn't necessarily. A low mood can be a stubborn thing. Recognition, however, is a crucial first step that will give you some composure and make it less likely that the lousy feeling will persist any longer than necessary.

As easy as it is to fall out of a natural good state of mind, what's amazing is that, in principle, it's just as easy to fall back in. Imagine a basketball in a swimming pool. The ball has natural buoyancy, which makes it constantly float to the surface. Holding the ball under the water takes effort, just like pressured thinking. If you stop holding the basketball down, it will float to the surface. Likewise, as your thinking relaxes, you will return to a natural state of equanimity. Recovering your state of mind isn't as much about doing something to get somewhere new as it is about letting go so you can get back to where you started. Obviously, this is different from other areas of life—for example, exercise—where creating change requires us to do more, not less. To gain the feeling of the Insight State of Mind, you need only let your inherent righting mechanism do its natural work. Your mood, like an unhanded basketball, will float to the surface with no further help from you. Relax and let the quiet mind return. Look for the good feeling. Everything else will take care of itself.

Robin likes to describe his indicators as being like the "idiot lights" on the dashboard of his car. Lost the good feeling? Red light on! As with dashboard lights, this mechanism is not foolproof. You will get into trouble if you forget to look at them, as anyone who's inadvertently run out of gas can attest. Over time, he has identified enough indicators to acquire a level of redundancy: if he misses one, he will probably notice another.

We all have different ways of letting go of the basketball. Young children are really good at it because they haven't formed the habit of holding on to thoughts. If you are a child whose world is falling apart because someone took your toy but then you hear that chicken fingers are for dinner, your mental world becomes chicken fingers, and the upsetting thoughts are gone. As adults, we are disadvantaged as we spend most of our lives in systems that train us to hold on to the basketball. This capacity is essential for sound analytic thinking, but just like using thoughts from our memory bank, we create problems when we use it to excess.

It's the *Art* of Insight, Not Just Technique

We do all sorts of things to get into an Insight State of Mind. Some people like to go for a walk or a run, and some take a vacation, garden, or pray. Some of us lie quietly on the sofa, relax in long baths, or wail on a saxophone. When we find ourselves stuck in a bad state of mind at the office, simply standing and stretching or going to a window and watching the clouds can do the trick. One of our executive clients gets her best insights after going to the movies. By her own admission, she has a very busy mind. When she goes to the movies, she gets caught up in the visual experience. She gets distracted from her habitual thinking, and her basketball floats to the surface.

Another client stands up and walks around when his thinking is blocked and he wants to get unstuck, while a third sits quietly by himself and writes in a notepad.

Any and all of these actions may work, but none work for everyone all the time, and if a single panacea existed, it would have been discovered by now. Certain methods may be useful, but they will be specific to you, and you should use them whenever it feels right rather than routinely or by prescription. It's also important not to get attached to one particular method. For any technique you discover or mental rule you form, you may find the opposite works just as well at other times. Those of us who favor concrete techniques and prescriptions must be careful lest our preferences interfere with returning to an Insight State of Mind.

Reliable access to insight is gained more through an understanding of and a sensitivity to a set of overarching principles than through adherence to a set of techniques. The appropriate method to access an Insight State of Mind in this moment comes naturally and extemporaneously, as in sports or in the arts. It has much more to do with getting your thinking out of the way and getting yourself into the present moment. What are you experiencing right now? Great basketball players like Bill Russell have an intrinsic understanding of the principles, rules, strategies, and mechanics of their game, but their play is dictated by what is required in the moment, often without

> Reliable access to insight is gained more through an understanding of and sensitivity to a set of overarching principles than through adherence to a set of techniques.

conscious thought on the part of the players. The Art of Insight is the same way.

For some of us, this shift of habit will occur quickly, while for others it will take more time. For Malcolm, becoming more conscious of his state of mind occurred over a number of years. During that time, he adopted faith in what he calls his *inner wisdom*. As this faith developed, Malcolm became more and more trusting that he would pick up on what was most important, confident that his inner wisdom would bring it to his attention when required. Others find that the shift requires attention, patience, and practice. Thankfully, the practice is not onerous. It feels good physically and psychologically and is accompanied by creative ideas, fewer mistakes, and sound judgment. Simply live your life and do your best to find your way to the good feeling.

Having an insight is the most natural occurrence in the world. Every day, when we discover things we don't know, we are having minor insights and realizations. Generating more insights doesn't require great effort; in fact, as we've explained, effort can be counterproductive. We need only recognize the state of mind in which insights are most likely to occur and find our way there more regularly. The Insight State of Mind doesn't include a lot of internal monologues. It is not a state where you stop thinking, but it is a state where you are not working hard on your thinking. Techniques aren't necessary to reach the Insight State of Mind. Again, you simply pay attention to the presence or absence of the feeling you associate with your best state of mind. Although your proficiency may have fallen due to neglect, none of this is new. You must simply reacquaint yourself with this natural, inborn capacity. If you step back and look for the good feeling, good thinking will follow. The change may not be instantaneous, but it will be reliable.

3 Insight Listening

Whether you have insights more frequently on your own or with others, one type of listening is particularly conducive to having insights. It is a key component to The Art of Insight, and it, too, is more a state of mind than a process. We refer to it as Insight Listening.

Everyone we've worked with has derived some value from learning to listen for insights. Based on reports from our clients, insights routinely occur during conversation. They occur in conversations between individuals, in small groups, or even in your head while you are talking to yourself. Listening to talk radio during a morning commute can spark an insight, but so can sitting through a boring sales pitch. In fact, you don't even need to be a participant in the conversation for it to trigger an insight. It turns out that *it is all about how we listen.*

Having more insights boils down to two things: being a bit disciplined to look for them and noticing the presence or absence of the feeling that is indicative of an Insight State of Mind. While both of these are simple in concept, unless you are graced with the disposition of a yogi, time and mindfulness are required to help cultivate these states.

No single path or technique will lead you to an Insight State of Mind without fail; however, Insight Listening may be the best chance you've got because it promotes a suspension of overthinking. When we employ Insight Listening, we are utilizing a skill that amplifies the probability that insights will occur by pointing us toward the Insight State of Mind.

In previous chapters, we have cautioned against the overuse of employing techniques as a way of achieving an Insight State of Mind. Over the years, we have found that, on occasion, we all find techniques that we think are useful but that in most cases will become less reliable over time. Our thinking is what keeps us from an Insight State of Mind, and employing techniques and methods generally requires additional conscious thought, which is exactly what we don't want for insights. Otherwise, this amounts to using thinking to combat thinking, and having such duels in one's head at the same time can be difficult.

To the extent that you can find value in a method or technique that helps you achieve an insightful state, use it, but ultimately you should be looking for something less mechanical and more lasting. You should be looking for the omnipresent connection to your inner wisdom that will guide you to where you need to go. Look for the state of mind that will foster the spontaneous generation of whatever thought, insight, or idea you need in that moment and you will be pleased with the results. When you notice you are overthinking, more often than not the simple recognition that unconscious thoughts are present is enough to allow the mind to relax and become more receptive to insights once again.

How to Listen to Others

It turns out that there are lots of ways of listening. We often try to commit to memory everything a person is saying so that we will be prepared afterward to accurately repeat everything he just said. We are taught to listen this way from a very early age in school, but when we do so, we leave little room for our own original thoughts. Other times we compare what we hear to what we already know. ("Does this person have a good point here, or is it really hogwash?") More often than we would like to admit, we are often really only partially listening. All this amounts to listening for content. We hold thoughts in our heads, thinking and reasoning about what we hear. We get so wrapped up in listening to our own thoughts, preparing our next point or our counterargument, that we miss out on the core of what is being said. Occasionally we get so distracted by our own thoughts that we hardly listen at all and end up daydreaming, clueless about what the person has just said. In each of these cases, thinking is active and engaged with a separate conversation occurring in our heads.

Insight Listening is a naturally occurring state that is more about being present and reflective than being active and engaged. When you listen for insight, you are emptying the clutter in your head and looking for fresh thoughts. You should not be deliberately exercising your intellect, trying to figure things out, or deciding what's most important. With practice, you'll be able to use this type of listening to hear more richly and think more creatively. The state is akin to listening to music. When little or nothing is on your mind, the music can touch you, but if you overthink it, it won't. Listening for insights is similar. The idea is to let the words wash over you without getting attached to any of your thoughts. Ideally, your mind should operate in a comfortable idle. You are not thinking, taking action, or reacting to what you are hearing. When we listen for content, we hold thoughts in our conscious mind, often to the point that we are incapable of allowing new thoughts to occur. With Insight Listening, you disengage the intellect and allow the detailed content of the words to fall away. In this form of listening, nothing in particular sticks; it is all just absorbed, and whatever is most important will spring to mind in the form of an insight.

The state of Insight Listening is not unlike the experience of watching a good movie for the first time. We enjoy the movie because we allow ourselves to drop our thinking and get carried off into the plot. If you watch a movie like a film critic and spend your energy thinking about the quality of the cast, costumes, and lighting, you will miss out on what is most important: the experience of being transported to a different time and place. The same experience happens if you go to a concert, read a novel, or look at a painting. You have one experience when you are actively analyzing and a completely different one when you are not. Nothing is wrong with intellectualizing these events, but unless you allow yourself to be present and transported by them, don't expect to have as robust an emotional experience. The best way to facilitate an insight is to stop your intellect from taking over your thoughts from a reflective, movie-watching state. This is Insight Listening.

Our colleague Ken Manning describes it this way:

One way we talk about listening is that it is something that we *do*—like we take personal credit for the
phenomenon. But listening is occurring on its own,
just like the heart beating, just like seeing. I can say
I am seeing and I can even direct that experience,
but seeing is happening anyway. It's the same with
listening. It's a natural function that occurs whether
directed or not.

Insight Listening and Fresh Thoughts

The underlying purpose of Insight Listening is to promote
an Insight State of Mind, where fresh thoughts and therefore
insights will abound. We will talk more specifically about listening for fresh thoughts below, but keep in mind as you work
through the exercises in this chapter that this is the ultimate
goal. The more fresh thoughts you have, the greater the chance
of an insight hitting. The practice of Insight Listening is about
training yourself to think freshly, to identify the feeling of fresh
thoughts and an Insight State of Mind and, of course, to recognize the all-important arrival of an insight.

Practicing Insight Listening

Over the years, we have used several different approaches to
teaching Insight Listening to our clients. For many, listening to
our own thoughts is the hardest thing to do—probably because
it is hard to police our own thinking. So we will begin with
settings that for most are somewhat easier.

A great time to practice is when you are with a large group of people and unlikely to be noticed. This could be when you are listening to a concert, play, movie, speech, sermon, or class lecture. You can run short training sessions with yourself. Practice Insight Listening for one minute, then shift to content listening, and then shift back and forth. This will let you develop fluency in both modes, as well as familiarity with the feeling of Insight Listening.

As you are Insight Listening, try disregarding the speaker's content and instead concentrate on discerning the feeling behind the words. Get used to being aware of the feeling of the situation: what sort of state of mind is it inducing in you? Is it elevating? Depressing? Fear inducing? Neutral? Using your own state of mind as a barometer can be helpful in a number of ways. It gives you information about how the other person is thinking. It can help keep you from becoming immersed in your own memory thinking or getting too caught up in the situation. This will lead to the greater likelihood of your having an insight.

Become aware of your current thinking. Are you deliberately moving thoughts around? Do you have lots of thoughts running through your head? This is not uncommon. Try for a while to think about not thinking. It can be awkward, but with a little practice, it will become easier. For a few minutes, slow the stream of thoughts in your head so that you aren't producing quite so much food for your brain to nosh on. Then, again, try to slow the thinking for an even longer stretch.

The thoughts that are constantly popping into our heads come from the combined experiences and memories of our lives. They show up unannounced and at times leave just as quickly, but when we hold on to one of these thoughts, when we feel its weight and toss it around for a bit, it tends to dominate our minds. Nothing is wrong with this, of course, if we are interested only in our past experiences, but if we are looking for a new idea, we must be able to drop these thoughts and not get wrapped up in them. As you become more aware of your thinking, discarding thoughts

> The ability to let go of conscious thinking widens the natural spaces between thoughts so that new ideas can surface.

will become more automatic. The ability to let go of conscious thinking widens the natural spaces between thoughts so that new ideas can surface.

One oft-forgotten fact is that it takes energy to think. While practicing Insight Listening and dropping thoughts, try to simply switch off the energy that you would normally use to think. This is definitely a "less is more" methodology. Remember, our natural state is an insightful one, so strip away the nonsense, leave the thick deliberation to the past, and just be in the moment.

If you find on occasion that this just won't work, don't be discouraged. Everyone has times when the busy mind takes over.

Now practice dropping thoughts. As soon as you notice that you're deliberately thinking about something, say to yourself, "I'm going to stop thinking about that." Stop thinking about it, but don't do so by putting another thought in its place. Don't put anything in its place; just appreciate the moment of nothingness, however brief it may be.

Don't concentrate too hard on any of this. A part of you knows how to do this better than your intellect, and you're not learning how to do anything you don't already know how to do. Instead, just throw yourself into it, and you'll get it eventually. You'll know you're on the right track if you are enjoying the good feeling of the Insight State of Mind. Try it and see. You'll develop comfort, and eventually faith, in it.

Practicing in smaller meetings with several people is great as well, provided you are careful not to look like you are day-dreaming. A good strategy for this type of setting is to adopt a posture of rapt attention. One way to do this is to make deep eye contact with the person who is speaking. Another is to shift your focus between the speaker's eyes and a strand of hair on her head. In either case, instead of trying to follow the content of what the person is saying, you should look more deeply into the feeling of what she is saying. You'll be "listening for" the feeling of the Insight State of Mind and for insights, and the speaker will never know it.

The danger with practicing this in smaller groups is that you might get discovered. If you are asked in some way to re-peat back what has just been said ("Larry, what do you think about that?"), the first thing that you want to do is pause and look for a fresh thought. If you have been daydreaming about something else entirely, it's probably not a good idea to share that fact. Instead, the new thought that you are looking for is about the subject that the person has been speaking on (which you are subconsciously aware of, if not consciously). To avoid an awkward silence, you might state the truth. "Well, I'm just reflecting on what you were saying." One of two things will then be true. Either you won't have anything original to add at the moment, or you will share your fresh thought.

Practicing Insight Listening with One Other Person

One of the most effective methods for practicing Insight Listening is to do so deliberately with one other person. In one-on-one Insight Listening, both parties are informed and fully enrolled in the process and the result is entirely different from normal conversations.

Below are some simple exercises you can practice with a friend or colleague. Video demonstrations are available on our website, TAOI Online Learning. We have found that it is generally easier to grasp the approach of TAOI when you are working with another person. On the other hand, you may find that recruiting a partner to practice with is more work than you would like to undertake right now. If this is the case, then read through the next few sections to get a sense of how these paired conversations should unfold, and then practice with an unsuspecting partner, but be sensitive to the fact that the other person isn't in on your little game.

EXERCISE:
Listening with Nothing on Your Mind

OVERVIEW

The objective of this exercise is to be present with your partner and her thinking with as little of your own thinking going on as possible.

PREPARATION

First, review with each other the purpose of the practice session, which is for the listener to listen with none of her own thinking going on to the extent possible. It helps to start out by taking a moment to discuss what the terms *insight* and *fresh thought* mean to you. This will help naturally point you toward an insightful state. Finally, you should take a moment to describe to each other what an Insight State of Mind feels like so that you will notice when it arrives. This important process serves to bait the hook and aim your unconscious mind in a productive direction.

THE EXERCISE

There are two roles (one speaker and one listener). Choose who will start out as the speaker, and have the listener monitor the time.

The speaker should take three minutes to describe a topic he is interested in. It can be something he is excited about, like his daughter's soccer game, or something he's recently enjoyed, like a movie or a new restaurant. For this exercise, it's best not to use a problem that is inherently mood lowering. Instead, the speaker should focus on a current business or personal issue on which he would like an insight. The listener should listen with nothing on her mind. That is to say, whenever the listener has an old thought or association about the topic being described, she should drop that thought and return to Insight Listening. For the most part, the listener should stay quiet, both verbally and mentally. Many people find this to be a challenge.

It is important that both partners keep their fingers on the pulse of the feeling of the conversation. If it drifts away from a good feeling, one of them should mention this so they can find their way back.

After the three minutes is up, take a few minutes for the listener to answer the following:

- What was that like? How did it feel?
- How much of the time were you able to remain mentally quiet?
- If you got caught up in your own thoughts, what happened? How did you find your way back (if you did)?

Occasionally during this exercise, you may encounter an awkward silence. Don't be discouraged; this is common the first time around! Soon you'll notice that the pauses encourage Insight Listening and allow space for fresh thoughts to arrive.

Switch roles so that you each get a chance to play both roles. By the end, you should have a better handle on listening with nothing on your mind. As you progress through the rest of the exercises we share with you in this chapter, you will find this getting easier.

Distractions and Dropping Thoughts

Almost inevitably at some point, you will notice yourself having a conversation in your head. When this happens, try to set it aside and return to empty-mindedness. These internal conversations interfere with the occurrence of insight. It's easy to get carried away by a fresh thought and go off on your own line of thinking. If you catch yourself doing this, stop and go back to listening with nothing on your mind. This may seem and often is challenging, yet we do it all the time. Imagine you are in the middle of a horrendous fight with someone when the phone rings. Are you going to pick up the phone and fight with whoever is on the line? Of course not. You switch your thinking; it's both automatic and unconscious. Another example of this might be if you've just finished a troublesome phone call. Your adrenaline is still pumping and you are distraught. Perhaps you've hung up furious at the caller. With your next appointment waiting in the hall, you might take a minute, breathe deeply, and settle down. When you start your meeting, you might even mention how wound up you are and excuse yourself for being a bit distracted at the moment.

One manager, in the middle of a very ugly lawsuit, found himself incessantly stewing over the suit, furious at what the other party was doing and concerned with how he was going to defend himself and retaliate. On his morning walk, he noticed that he was boiling again about the lawsuit and annoyed at how it had taken over his thinking. He consciously pushed all thoughts of the suit out of his mind and committed himself to not ruining his walk by agonizing over it. Not two minutes later, he was completely consumed by these thoughts again. He recommitted to dropping all thoughts about the suit, but a few minutes later, he was caught up once again. This pattern continued for a while, and each time he would redouble his efforts, trying not to be seduced by the dialogue going on in his head.

Then something odd happened. He was enjoying himself and the glorious nature around him on his walk. It had been twenty minutes or more since he had thought about the lawsuit.

To this day, he is not clear about what specifically happened in his thinking. The unwanted thinking probably wasn't banished, but at the same time, small moments of clarity were slowly finding a beachhead, expanding at each iteration. Whatever the case, his disciplined practice seemed to be a factor. Each moment of clarity enabled him to remember that equanimity was possible, even if only fleeting. From then on, even though thoughts of the lawsuit frequently returned, they no longer gripped his thinking in the same way. Years after this occurrence, this man still gets caught up in thought storms on occasion, but he knows that they are by their very nature temporary, and so he is no longer imprisoned by them.

Incidentally, bad thoughts are not the only thing that can be distracting. Our friend Terry Ann describes how fresh thoughts can derail you as well.

My inclination can be to get swept up with fresh thoughts, even when I'm really trying to listen and be totally present in a conversation. This phenomenon is more clear and less problematic when I'm walking along the river by myself or peacefully listening to an audiobook. Suddenly, I've checked out of the book as thoughts tumble one after another into my mind. They're usually new thoughts and are relevant to something I have been thinking about, and while this is a good thing, I don't hear the book anymore, even though it's still playing in my headphones. When the thoughts stop, I check back into the book, and I have to rewind because I have heard nothing. When I'm on my own, this is exciting and great, but when it happens in a conversation, it is not necessarily so.

Be alert to what you allow yourself to take in with your listening. You don't have to "do" Insight Listening as much as you step back and let it occur without interfering with it. It's like lying on the beach with nothing in particular on your mind and then something comes along that distracts you. If you get upset about being distracted, the distraction will grow, and you will wind up in a messy conversation with yourself about the distraction. Your other option is to wave as it passes by and return to your beautiful day at the beach, blissfully present.

EXERCISE:

Fresh Thought Hunt

OVERVIEW

You may be wondering when you get to listen for insights. Soon, we promise, but there's one last thing we'd like to cover: learning to listen for fresh thoughts. In this exercise, don't worry about whether you are having an insight or not. Just get familiar with noticing the arrival of fresh thoughts. The insights will take care of themselves. If you are focused on trying to create an insight, you are actually working your mind, and this will interfere with insight generation.

Instead, get comfortable with inviting fresh thoughts in. Odds are that one of them will be an insight. The better you get at pointing your awareness in the direction of freshness and the unknown, the more likely you will hear the insight when it arrives. Video demonstrations are available on our website, TAOI Online Learning.

Listening for fresh thoughts has a certain intentionality to it, but it is not hard work like most conscious actions. It's more akin to reading a book, watching a play, or listening to music.

> Listening for fresh thoughts is akin to reading a book, watching a play, or listening to music.

PREPARATION

In this exercise, you will practice with a partner, listening for fresh thoughts. First, go over the ground rules and be clear on the purpose of the practice session, which is to generate as many fresh thoughts as possible and to notice the feeling that accompanies each when it arrives. It's a good idea to take a moment to discuss what the terms *insight* and *fresh thought* mean to you. This naturally steers you toward an insightful state. Finally, take a moment to describe to each other what an Insight State of Mind feels like so that you will notice when it arrives.

THE EXERCISE

There are two roles (one speaker and one listener). Choose who will start out as the speaker, and have the listener monitor the time.

Part 1

The speaker should describe to the listener a current business or personal issue on which he would like an insight. Take *only two minutes* to describe the situation; more time than this will get in the way. While the listener listens, she should do so with nothing on her mind. That is to say, whenever an old thought or association about the topic arises, it should be dropped, and the listener should return to Insight Listening.

Part 2

At this point, the speaker will go on a Fresh Thought Hunt. For three minutes, the speaker, to the best of his ability, should voice *only* fresh thoughts about the situation as they arise. This generally means that there will be lengthy pauses, followed by short phrases. This may feel a bit unusual as the cadence will be nothing like a normal conversation. Still, the speaker ground rules are simple: you are either voicing a fresh thought on the topic, or you are listening with nothing on your mind, looking for a thought that you have never had before.

During part 2, the listener should listen with nothing on her mind and notice when something strikes her as fresh. It might be something the speaker has said, but it might also be something that *she* has never thought before. In either case, a mental note should be made that something fresh happened. If something the speaker says strikes the listener as fresh, she might acknowledge it out loud ("Wow, that sounded really fresh"). This can help encourage the speaker, but for the most part, the listener should remain silent.

It is important that both partners keep their fingers on the pulse of the feeling of the conversation so that when it drifts away from a good feeling, one of them can mention this and they can find their way back.

Part 3
Once the speaker has concluded his three-minute Fresh Thought Hunt, together the partners should talk about what that experience was like. Both the speaker and the listener should share the items that they felt were fresh thoughts.

The three parts form one complete round of a Fresh Thought Hunt. If you like, at this point you can switch roles and repeat the exercise.

KEEP IN MIND
By the end of this exercise, you should have a pretty good idea of what a fresh thought feels like, and you should have further developed your ability to listen with nothing on your mind. Here's how it might look: You are listening to the speaker with nothing on your mind and feeling quiet, passive, reflective, and uncritical. You will likely enjoy what he has to say. When he says something fresh, you will feel it. It may not be an insight but if it is new for either of you, you will at least notice a difference from typical thought. Something behind what is being said will affect you. At this point, you will feel a pull to start actively thinking about what has just been said; avoid this and return to a quiet mind. Once again a fresh thought will appear, and you will get impacted. This will continue for

the duration of the exercise, and at some point, one of you may have a genuine insight.

EXERCISE:
Coaching for Fresh Thoughts and Insights

OVERVIEW

This exercise builds on the previous two and has two objectives. The first is for the speaker to have some fresh thoughts about something he is interested in. The second is for the listener to learn to coach and otherwise help the speaker have more fresh thoughts. Watch a video demonstration on our website, TAOI Learning Online.

PREPARATION

In this exercise, you will practice with a partner once again, this time listening for fresh thoughts and coaching for fresh thoughts. First, go over the ground rules and be clear on the purpose of the practice session. Also, before you begin, take a moment to describe to each other what an Insight State of Mind feels like so that you will notice when it arrives.

THE EXERCISE

There are two roles (one speaker and one listener). Choose who will start out as the speaker and have the listener monitor the time.

Part 1
The speaker should take two minutes to describe something he would like some fresh thought on or insight into.

The listener should listen with nothing on her mind. This sets the stage.

Part 2

The speaker now has four minutes to go on a Fresh Thought Hunt to look more deeply into what he wants. The listener will be the speaker's coach. She will again be listening with nothing on her mind as best she can.

The two parts form one complete round of the Coaching for Fresh Thoughts and Insights exercise. If you like, at this point you can switch roles and repeat the exercise.

KEEP IN MIND

Above all, when you're the listener/coach, you want to maintain rapport and be very careful of anything that feels confronting or that might add any sort of pressure on the speaker. You want to encourage the speaker to discover a new, fresh perspective on his desires. It's quite okay to ask questions about the speaker's thinking ("Was that a memory or a fresh thought?"), and it's also helpful to acknowledge when something the speaker says strikes you as fresh. You can offer a thought if it is truly fresh, but generally, coaching should be used sparingly.

Stay away from questions about the content or the specifics of the situation. Getting consumed in the content of the speaker's words will impede your ability to be helpful and spark insights. You may have been able to recite all the facts he had given you, and you may even be able to give him some advice or even your best answer for the situation, but there likely would have been no insight.

Don't screen the speaker's words with your intellect, or else you will screen the feeling out and probably the insights along with it. The practice of Insight Listening requires tuning in to what lies beyond the speaker's words. What is he really communicating? The feeling of the conversation is as important as its content.

Do not offer anything that remotely resembles advice. Do not try to solve the speaker's problem or offer solutions of your own, no matter how good your idea may be. You can do that after the exercise is over. When you try to solve a problem, more often than not, you are consciously accessing memory and trying to fit pieces together. Perhaps more importantly, you are working within the framing your partner has provided you. You want to avoid that kind of limit. You might end up offering a fresh thought that's out of left field and seemingly irrelevant, but it might be just the thing that triggers an important insight in your partner.

You may need to gently interrupt the speaker if he goes off on a memory-based thought train. You might say something like, "Pause for just a second, Jim." Here are other phrases you might find helpful: "Give me another fresh thought about that." "What's another way of looking at this?" "What's a question you have about that?" "I'm wondering what you are thinking right now." And our personal favorite: "If you weren't thinking whatever you're thinking right now, what would you be thinking?"

Even though you are not deliberately listening to the content, you will often realize that the speaker has related certain facts that seem at odds with each other. If you gently ask about the contradiction, he too may see the discrepancy, which may be at the root of his inability to find a solution. Often the challenge is not in the reality of the situation but in how it's being thought of. Or you may pick up on what seems to you to be a missing piece to the puzzle, and by mentioning the missing piece, the speaker can make new connections and follow a fresh train of thought.

Imagine for a moment that you are the listener/coach and your partner is a few minutes into reporting the details of his situation. As he is describing the complexity that makes the problem hard to solve, you listen without paying close attention to the details or content. Instead of the content of his description, what registers inside you is his frustration. When you mention this fact, your partner feels somehow relieved. He says, "Gee, that's right. Thanks for seeing that." The rapport between you increases, and his mind settles down. The subject of the conversation has actually changed. The listener might ask, "Well, what do you think about that frustration?" Hopefully, something will occur to the speaker that mitigates his frustration, and if you're lucky, he may have a lasting insight into his original problem.

The amount of conversation management depends very much on the context and aim of the conversation. When listening this way with his children, one colleague sits down, connects, and listens deeply for whatever comes to him. To the extent that he has an agenda, it's only to be with the children, not to look for an insight. When he's on a business call with a client who has a specific problem, then the goal is absolutely to look for an insight. Listening with that in mind, he will frame the conversation and question based on whatever feels fresh and relevant in that moment.

Insight Listening Conversations

Now you have the basics of how to listen for insights and how to help others have more insights. You may have gathered by now that conducting conversations with such a limited structure doesn't require much management at all. The key is to keep a good feeling and let your wisdom take over. Your goal is never to solve the other person's problem. It's his issue, and you should be appreciating and reinforcing his insights more than your own. You will of course still have some of your own fresh thoughts, and occasionally they will be insights. Primarily, you are listening to him, however. When you are open and interested, your partner is most likely to have an insight. Don't consciously think about what you're doing. When you are connected to your deepest wisdom, you will operate on autopilot. You will know when to speak and when to be silent (which should be most of the time). You will soon discover that both what you do and what you don't do are of equal importance. When you speak, you won't be rehearsing or overthinking what you say. Instead, your speech should feel quiet, reflective, and spontaneous, as if the words were traveling through you. This manner of speaking will elevate your rapport with the person. In fact, the more you speak this way, in any setting, the more people will be drawn to hearing what you have to say.

Our friend Ed likes to describe a camping trip with his family when his son asked him to go fishing with him. The thing is, Ed doesn't fish. His job, as he describes it, was to sit quietly next to his son as his son fished because that helped his son. All his son wanted him to do was to sit there. He says, "There is something about presence that helps us find the fish."

Because the listener is in a reflective, uncritical state, she hears more deeply than she might otherwise and is able to see the essence of the problem being expressed. Not only that, but because she isn't hung up in intellectual thinking, she is free to have deep insights that either solve the problem or help her partner see it in a completely new light. A deep insight into a problem permanently changes the way we look at it, and when we have a new perspective, a clear solution will present itself, often in days or even hours.

Content listening, too, may result only in an able recitation of the facts and perhaps even some sound advice based on past experience, but it is less likely to generate any real insight into the problem.

With Insight Listening, whether you're the speaker or the listener, your mind is free to operate like a radio that doesn't care about what station it's receiving. Authors and coaches Richard Carlson and Joseph Bailey describe it this way:

> It's receiving all the incoming data without analyzing, processing, or rejecting it. In free-flowing mode you don't interpret from a belief system, you don't judge, and you don't anticipate what will be said next. You simply listen nonjudgmentally, trying to take in what the other person is saying. . . . You allow yourself to be affected by the essence of what the other person is saying—not by the words but by the feelings behind the words. . . . You are not distracted with other thoughts or memories that have been triggered by the conversation. You have no agenda, no expectations, no outcome in mind.[1]

You would think that looking beyond the words would hamper your ability to remember what has been said, but because your subconscious discerns what is most important, you are actually able to recall the most crucial points. You might think you would succumb to boredom, but if you are fully present and not caught up in your own thoughts, you will find what your partner is saying is very interesting. If you don't find the person engaging, then it's not him; it's your thinking. One consequence of Insight Listening is that you become far more likely to enjoy what the other is saying. Because you are no longer preoccupied by your own thoughts and agenda, you become absorbed in the spirit of what is being said, which—without fail—is more interesting than what you would have heard otherwise.

Insight Listening with a Person Unfamiliar with Insight Listening

Now let's deal with TAOI in the real world. You will, of course, use everything that you've learned in the previous exercises. With someone who has experience in TAOI, you can simply employ the methods overtly, while focusing on questions that you both are interested in.

The Art of Insight When You Are Seeking an Insight

When you are working with someone who is unfamiliar with TAOI and your aim is to look for your own insights, you need to keep a few things in mind. The approach is similar to the one used when you were practicing Insight Listening in a small group. Your aim should be mindful attention, listening with nothing on your mind. You want to look for the good feeling and, of course, listen for your own fresh thoughts. Don't worry about your partner being disturbed by the fact that you have nothing on your mind. Expect instead that quite the opposite will occur. Invariably, your partner will feel more deeply listened to than in other conversations. That being said, your partner may be puzzled by the frequency with which you choose to pause and reflect, particularly if this hasn't been your speaking style in the past. If you have good rapport with your partner, you will sense this and might find it appropriate to explain what you are doing and why, particularly if you feel that your listening is somehow hindering your partner's experience.

There is a very good chance, if not almost certainty, that your partner will start to give you advice. As you probably now know, this won't feel good, and you won't like it as compared to the feeling and quality of the conversations you had in the exercises. Some people never really enjoy the experience of getting advice, even when they recognize the potential value in the solutions being offered. We hope that with practice, you will see why a conversation full of fresh thoughts is so different.

Be prepared. It's going to be a challenge to deal with the good ideas born largely from memory about what you should do in your situation. Some of them might actually be good ideas and even fresh for you. But others, perhaps most of them, will feel stale and, if you're not careful, can diminish whatever good feeling you may currently be enjoying. Don't let this happen! You know the feeling you'd like to have. Let your thinking be gentle, and maintain your equanimity.

We'd like to promise that if you are mentally quiet enough, eventually your partner will settle down and stop offering advice, but we all know people who tend to live in their heads. You notice them because they think and talk very fast, and you feel you have to think and talk very fast to keep up with them. When these folks walk out of your office, their fast-talking, busy mind-set doesn't stop and probably won't unless it gets some attention. One time, Malcolm sat in dead silence for forty-five minutes quietly listening to a colleague advise him on what to do with a situation he had just described.

> I was perfectly happy as I listened, and after about ten minutes or so, I got really interested in how long this guy could continue. I figured that if I stayed in a good state of mind, for sure I'd have an insight or two, but I never did. Finally after forty-five minutes of not having said a single word or offering a hint of encouraging body language, I called a halt to it by shifting the topic. I'm sure that he would have gone on much longer. The good news was that I was still in a good place. It had been a great experiment and solid practice on maintaining my Insight State of Mind.

As a general rule, this sort of session is hardly a good use of time for either individual. You should gently interrupt the conversation and put it back on the track of sharing fresh thoughts. Try asking the person to offer a solution that he has never thought of before, something outside his usual approach. Try other ways to steer him into fresh thought territory. Although not ideal, some situations call for you to be directive and to gently but firmly steer the conversation. You have a right to do this since this conversation is presumably about helping you, and you should specify what you want and need. In this case, only fresh thoughts!

TAOI When You Are Trying to Help Someone Have an Insight

If your purpose is to help facilitate an insight for a partner who is not aware that you are using Insight Thinking, the approach is not much different from the previously discussed exercise where two people are looking for insights together. The trick is to focus the conversation on getting your partner to generate as much fresh thought as possible, while avoiding ideas that have been said in the past. During the conversation, you may find it helpful to interrupt your partner if she is getting caught up in her memory and ask her directly for a fresh thought that she has not considered before. If you listen insightfully and maintain good rapport, you will find that your presence will be a strong catalyst for her insights. While she might initially be confused at the tack you are taking, she will quickly start to generate new ideas. If your partner gets stuck, then you can offer a fresh thought of your own. It will illustrate what a fresh thought looks like, and it will be an example of the feeling that accompanies the Insight State of Mind. Your partner may feel helped by the thought itself, or it may serve to trigger her own fresh thought or unblock a mental logjam. As with all these exercises, the key is to always maintain rapport.

Insight Listening to Yourself

So far, we've focused on Insight Listening with others. Let's begin by acknowledging that going on an insight hunt when you have no one to play with can be more difficult. That said, a number of things can help you have insights while you are on your own.

As we have stressed, you want to be looking for the feeling associated with your Insight State of Mind. Occasionally, a run or relaxed shower will be just what you need to set the stage. You want to stay in that easygoing, curious state, alert for incoming insights. The challenge is to be mindful of either the absence or the presence of the good feeling. It's not necessary to plan much beyond this, but with a bit of diligent practice, maintaining this state will become easier to the point that it becomes normal. Remember that you are on an insight hunt and you can always use intuition to direct your next step on that hunt.

When writing, you can either be analytic—rearranging ideas and words, editing sentences, and constructing arguments—or use free association, a journaling approach, and stream of consciousness. When praying or meditating, you can either follow strict rituals—reciting scripture or actively praying for a specific purpose—or have a reflective conversation with your inner wisdom or higher power and invite it in. When engaged in strenuous physical activity or a leisurely stroll on the beach, you can be either mentally active or mentally idle. When talking to yourself, you can engage either in active self-talk with intentional visualization or a contemplative conversation between you and yourself. While insights can happen in either one or the other of these modes in each case, they will happen more readily in the latter.

One important distinction to be made is that it is absolutely possible to hold something in your attention without doing any mental work on it. If you're looking out the window at a beautiful vista, you're very likely not counting the trees or comparing the shades of the rocks; you are simply looking at the scene. If you are on a walk, you may be conscious of obstacles on the ground, but these remain in the background of your thinking unless the obstacles become dangerous or suddenly relevant. When you take a shower, you are executing a series of tasks, but for the most part they don't take much active thinking. You are largely present and aware, and although you may be doing some low-level thinking, it isn't hard work, and you don't have to do anything with these thoughts. Instead, your mind is in a clear, gentle, fertile state, ready for something new to appear.

In all these settings, you are listening for an insight. The idea is not to actively grasp at insights but to softly invite them in. It may help to hold the subject in your attention, but don't try to do anything with it. If you get a thought about the subject, just let the thought flow by. Don't deliberately build on it and make it into another thought, which would only serve to set off what we call a *train of thought*. If the thought seems to build organically on its own accord, then perhaps allow this to happen, but don't go out of your way to try to make this happen. If another thought pops up, let that one flow by, too. Put all your mental tools back in their drawers; nothing is needed to work on the topic. The subject is simply there, nothing more. At a minimum, this experience will be very restful, even if you don't get any insights.

For many of us, the gears of our thinking are so well polished that when they are grinding, they don't make that much noise. We think that we are being reflective when actually our mental motor is revved up—just very quietly. When nothing insightful shows up, we have a tendency to fabricate something with quiet analytical thinking that looks to us like reflection but in fact is something else entirely. This is why for many, if not most, of us, learning to listen for insights on our own can be challenging. Listening for insights requires diligence and may be a lot easier to learn with others because then less dueling occurs with our own internal mechanisms. The better you get at this practice with other people, the more quickly your capacity and sensitivity will leak into your ability to listen to yourself.

Some people are more inclined to have insights when they walk in the woods or are otherwise by themselves in the outdoors. Other people are more inclined to have insights during conversations with other people when there is abundant activity. There is no reason to believe that one instance is any better than the other, but the question for you is, what is going on in the moment? Are you in a mentally bound mind-set, or are you open and easygoing?

Remember that none of these rules is hard and fast. Sometimes you might feel the need to deliberately build on a thought you just had, and this might be precisely what is needed in that moment. The fact is, when you are unpressured in your thinking, you exert mental muscles mindfully, not habitually, and you will know the difference by the way it feels.

All of us have our own kinds of internal dialogues: some of them lead to insights, and some of them don't. Here's an example from one of our clients:

When I'm actively thinking about a topic, it actually seems like I'm in a conversation with myself in my head. Sometimes it shows up as two people talking, both of whom are me, with a third me sitting on the side, listening to the other two mes talk to each other. This resembles the friendly question-and-answer that occurs in the kind of conversation described in the earlier Insight Listening exercises between two people. The questioner asks some questions, makes observations about how the other me is thinking about the topic, and often spots contradictions in either the thinking or in the data. It's rather like the second me is helping the first me think better, with the third me observing it all.

A second mode I've noticed is when the conversation becomes more like a conversation between me and somebody else who's both me and beyond me. People of faith will recognize this capacity, although this is more like questions and explorations with a friend than perhaps receiving truth or wisdom from a higher source. I use this mode when writing. I ask, "What do you think about that?" and "What else have you said that you think is important?" Fresh thoughts tumble out, although, of course, not all are immediate insights. In both of these modes, the questions serve to push my thinking into the not known, the still undefined, either directly or by freshly questioning things that I think I know but may well not be true.

Of course, different people talk about these mental conversations in different terms. One of the most common is the "little voice in one's head." But people often don't distinguish more than one voice being active at the same time. Malcolm talks about having a "heady" voice that is loaded with intellectual content and an "insight voice" that to him seems to emerge from the ether. For him, there are not two voices together. His normal talking with himself is displaced by the "insight me" coming from the unknown. A lot of people have described their mental conversations along these lines. Yet another way we've heard this described is that thought is forming from a kind of word-free darkness. From that darkness an image starts to form, and at first you see something that isn't quite clear. Then as you continue to look, a moment comes when it becomes clear and you are able to describe what you are seeing. In this case, it's about getting an inkling that sharpens into focus over a relatively short period of time. Ultimately, what you find yourself doing is trying to describe in words what you have seen.

You may have a completely different way of describing these conversations in your head, and you may not relate to these descriptions at all. We don't think there is much value in considering any of this too much, except to say that it may be useful for you to be mindful of your preferred style. While you don't want to overplan or overmanage, it can help to be deliberate and to carve out uninterrupted time for each mode so that you can listen insightfully to each voice. Without this deliberate intention, the world can quickly crowd out any time you might have had to operate in your preferred insightful state.

Listening for insight is simply about being present and reflective. It's a very natural, maybe even our most natural, way of listening, but it can be a bit awkward for many of us to empty the chatter in our heads and look instead for fresh thoughts. We have to recover our ability to drop distractions, allow the detailed content of the words to fall away, and instead, absorb the feeling of the communication, whether it be with another person or only with ourselves.

When we listen for fresh thoughts in this manner, insights ultimately hit.

All the discussions in this chapter on strategy and method really only make sense if you quiet your mind. You are not so much employing techniques as you are lightly observing your listening and thinking. Over time, this way of listening becomes spontaneous with insights happening all the time—we need only notice them.

4 Thinking into and out of an Insight-State of Mind

As newcomers consider the modes and methods we have described, they relate them to their personal experience and realize that this is the way that they already operate. They become curious as to how they can adjust the way they live to get into an Insight State of Mind with greater regularity.

Here is where things get interesting. It turns out that trying to get into an Insight State of Mind is a bit of a fool's errand. This insight state is actually our natural, default state. In an Insight State of Mind, our brains are not being overworked. Rather, they are relaxed, and nothing is more natural than finding your way to a state of relaxation. It is where most of us find ourselves right before we fall asleep each night, and it is where we find ourselves when we wake up each morning. Either a conscious or an unconscious effort is needed to move us out of our natural state. However, working hard at achieving an Insight State of Mind will not yield positive results.

In the 1980s, noted physician Dr. T. Berry Brazelton described the following six behavioral states of the newborn:

quiet sleep, active sleep, drowsiness, quiet alert, active awake, and crying. In the quiet alert state, the baby's eyes are wide open, bright, and shiny. There are few to no body movements, and the baby's energy is directed into seeing and hearing. Normal newborns spend two-thirds of the first hour of their lives in the quiet alert state, 30 percent in the crying state, and the rest in the other states. Many experts have concluded that the period between thirty and sixty minutes after birth is when the newborn is in the state of highest awareness and has the highest capacity for learning.[1]

The Insight State of Mind is actually our default state.

The babies studied weren't meditating or deliberately entering some type of deeper consciousness. They were just being present. Not until we become active, educated thinkers are we so easily diverted from what would otherwise be our natural, present, insightful state. This is important. Anytime you are not in an Insight State of Mind, it is because you have done some type of mental work (most likely unrecognizable by your conscious mind) to drive yourself out of it.

Remember the analogy of the basketball in the pool from chapter 2? You will never have to push the basketball to the surface, just as you will never have to think your way into an Insight State of Mind. Your mind will return to this state naturally and with little effort—as soon as you stop thinking your way out of it.

Since we can't stop thinking entirely, the answer is to relax and accept. Relax your thinking so that too many cafeteria trays don't pile up to the point that you can't see what's in front of your nose, and accept that thinking is constantly going on in the background and that eventually, when space allows, an insight will occur.

Thought Governs One's State of Mind

A couple we know shared a story with us about a trip they took to California to visit some friends. The family they were visiting had very small children, and when the couple got to their friends' house on the first morning, the situation was a bit chaotic. Our friend describes the experience:

> Our hosts had decided we would eat out that evening and asked us what time we would like to have dinner. We said that since we were on East Coast time, and have a difficult time digesting late at night, six would be great. They said sure. The chaos with the kids continued for a bit, but around eleven o'clock, we went to visit a local museum and finally sat down for lunch at around three. I remember thinking, "Geez, if I eat now, I am not going to want to eat again at six." I had a small snack to keep me until dinner. Our hosts had a full meal, and the whole time I was wondering how they would be hungry again in just a couple of hours. I dropped that thought and tried to relax. At this point, there was no question that my state of mind was deteriorating, but I had noticed this sort of thing before, so I made note of it and just tried to go with the flow.

When we finally did return to our friends' house, it was six thirty, and no one was getting ready to go to eat. Over an hour later, we left for dinner, but then we had to drop off the kids at a babysitter on the way. At this point, my expectations for a relaxing evening were completely blown and my mood sunk even lower than before. I was operating in damage control with all my shields up, ready to react to anything that might aggravate me. I realized that I was in a bad way, so I started to look (unsuccessfully) for ways to improve my state. For the rest of the evening this searching was the best that I could do. There wasn't anything I could do to improve my experience because the quality of my thinking was just too poor.

The following morning, I woke up to a beautiful sunny day, happy to be alive, with no concern for the previous evening.

When you discover, or even suspect, that you are in a low mood, the first point to remember is that while you often can't make your mood better, you can generally keep it from getting worse. How? Well, when you are emotionally agitated, the urge is to do something about it. The problem with this is that whatever action you take will be born of low-quality thought and is therefore unlikely to work. In fact, it may even make matters worse. In this situation, the better strategy is, as Dwight Eisenhower reportedly ordered, "Don't just do something; stand there," at least psychologically. Acknowledge that you've momentarily lost your bearings, and don't take any bait that carries a bad feeling or that might set you into a downward spiral. Patiently let your mind settle before doing anything or making any big decisions. Hopefully you can avoid taking action, but in the relatively few cases where you can't, try to do whatever carries the best feeling and then learn from the result.

Sleep is vastly underappreciated as a reset button for the brain. Sometimes your only option is to get a good night's sleep and to wait for the world to look better. When we are in a low state of mind, we may feel as though we will be stuck there forever, but our head will eventually clear itself without any work on our part.

At the time, our friend couldn't figure out how to snap himself out of his crummy state. He was, however, aware of the effect a low mood has on how he experiences and interacts with the world and was able in the interim to have a nice time with his friends.

> A few days after returning from our trip, I was on one of my morning walks, where I often get a lot of insights. It was a breezy New England day, and I suddenly realized that when our friends had asked us what time we wanted to have dinner, they didn't have any real intention of honoring that time. It was just a social nicety to express concern for our needs.
>
> I had a whole series of experiences that evening that were based on a reality that didn't exist. I was operating as though they had broken a promise to

me. My thoughts had bounced all over the place that afternoon, from wondering why my friends were so inconsiderate to being amazed that they could live such haphazard lives. In truth, they were perfectly courteous hosts. From their point of view, everything was fine, since they always like to go to dinner at seven thirty or eight. To them, the conversation about dinnertime had been an exchange of social pleasantries without any serious commitment.

In a low-quality state of mind, we take things far more personally than we would otherwise. Since our psychological experience is a consequence of how we are thinking, the bad moods that we find ourselves in are of our own creation, even if triggered by external circumstances. These circumstances, our families, our friends, and their antics, actually have nothing to do with how we feel. The perception that the world has conspired to ruin our experience is entirely in our heads. This sort of thing occurs all the time to varying degrees. We have a set of experiences and expectations from which we create a story around our present reality. Depending on the quality of our state of mind, that story can lead to drastically different conclusions. How the story plays out is entirely up to us.

It is impossible to live your entire life in a good mood. None of these concepts will keep you from ever having a bad day or slipping into a poor state of mind, but they will help build your resilience. We hope that when your state of mind starts to slip, instead of getting a full-blown cold, you'll only get a few sniffles.

Discovering the Importance of Thought

Shortly after graduating from college, Charlie was in a relationship with a woman that wasn't on the right track. Below he gives an account of the profound insight that was the genesis of his work at Innovation Associates and a long career pursuing high-quality thinking.

One evening, my fiancée and I went to the house of a couple we were friends with to have a bottle of wine. When we arrived, she started right in on me with a series of what I heard as really disparaging comments. I had a lot of self-control in moments like this, so I calmly asked her to stop. When she continued with the belittling remarks, I became increasingly upset, and this continued for the rest of our visit. On the ride home, our quarrel boiled into a series of loud accusations. She even denied saying anything derogatory. Now, not only was she being irrational, but she was being dishonest as well. I was furious. She was wrong, and I could prove it.

At home later, I was standing in the doorway to my home office when she sat down at my desk and started to cry. The seeming injustice overwhelmed me. After all the awful things she had said, she had the audacity to feel sorry for herself!

And then the entire world fell away, and I was left staring into empty space. I saw that my fiancée was not causing me to feel angry. I knew that there was no physical way she could be responsible. When she had spoken, sound waves traveled from her mouth to my ears, but there was no way that sound waves could make me feel. *It was my thinking! I realized that my thoughts were the entire source for my anger.*

I understood science and structure and equations of the natural world and the physical reality of things, but in this moment, I saw in a very profound way that my personal experience of the world was and is only a function of my own thinking. It wasn't an intellectual understanding but a deeply personal insight—well beyond any understanding I had ever experienced before.

After this insight, I had an utterly new appreciation for the power of thought. I recognized that with thought playing such an essential role, it was crucial to improve my thinking and that of my clients. This marked the start of a lifelong pursuit of high-quality thinking.

Over the years, we have learned that as effective as being vigilant about your thinking can be, it isn't as important as seeing how your thinking forms your psychological experience. Once this occurs, you will come to possess both a conscious and an unconscious awareness about how your thoughts affect your reality. Your mind will settle more easily, you will have insights more regularly, and when you do get stuck in a poor state of mind, it will be for a shorter period of time. In a phrase, you will become more psychologically resilient.

When we are disturbed, we lose our bearings, and our perception of reality gets cloudy. When you shake a snow globe, the snow swirls about for a while, but eventually it settles. Moods are similar. There is no question that your globe is going to be shaken from time to time. The more you understand that your thinking determines your psychological experience, the more quickly your snow will settle.

Practice Versus Technique

You may have, or want to have, a favorite technique to fix your head, but when you're caught in a bad mood, such techniques tend to be unreliable at best. An important distinction exists between a technique that you use to make something different in a specific situation and a practice that you try to employ on a regular basis.

Josh likes to swim. If he hits the pool in the morning, it sets up an entirely different day for him than when he does not. He comes out of that swim feeling great physically and in a terrific state of mind that often carries four or more hours into the day. Meetings run smoothly, business conversations are efficient, and participants enjoy great rapport. You may have your own version of Josh's swim, like running, yoga, cycling, or meditation. If so, you probably know the kind of feeling we are referring to.

Usually, during the course of those thirty minutes of rhythmic motion in the pool, Josh's mind settles. But what happens when he gets in a lousy mood and tries to swim to improve it? Well, let's tell you about Diane.

Diane is a senior editor of a business magazine. From time to time, she is given the opportunity to write an essay of her own. One time the deadline loomed and she had no idea for her essay. She packed her laptop, left the office, and went home to take a bath, because she always gets her insights in the bathtub.

She emerged from the tub and sat down at her computer, but no ideas showed up for the essay. She sat for a while, waiting for something to come along, but nothing happened. Diane headed back to the bathtub. Emerging with wrinkly fingers from the bath, she dried off and sat down at her desk, but after some time, no ideas for her essay had surfaced. Back into the tub she went. Then back to her desk. No ideas. Back to the tub again.

Luckily for her skin, Diane had an idea hit during her sixth bath.

A technique is something that you do in the hopes of changing your situation—in this case your state of mind. A practice is something that you do because you like the thing itself and, in our case, because it brings with it mental benefits. A practice doesn't carry the expectation that it will necessarily change a specific situation. Instead, the function of a practice is to remind you of what is available to you all the time. You know that the Insight State of Mind is possible because you experience it during or after your practice. Because you know that it is possible, you know that your loss is only temporary. And you know what you need to look for to find your way back.

Here's a friend describing how prayer works in his life:

I'm a little embarrassed to say that often my daily prayers kind of look like a list of things that I really hope God will give me. It's like little old me giving God a list of things that he should do. But that all changes when I get to "Thy will be done." Then it is no longer little old me. I am one with God. That feeling, of course, is inexpressible in words. But I am so lucky in that I can carry it into the rest of my day.

If you have a practice that brings you the kind of peace of mind that we associate with an Insight State of Mind, by all means keep it up. If you don't have one, you might think about starting one. But think of the state of mind that accompanies your practice as your normal state, not the one you just visit temporarily or as a consequence of disciplined work.

Many of us can draw a fairly sharp distinction between what we might call our work state of mind and our vacation state of mind, which we visit typically just on vacation. Since our vacation state of mind is infrequent and conditioned by the occurrence of a vacation, we think of it as an unusual state and our work state of mind as the regular state. It is true that for many of us, the work state of mind is the most common one, but it is not the most natural one.

The Role of Thought

Your psychological experience is governed by thought. Your states of mind (insight or otherwise) and mood are not caused by circumstances, although they generally appear to be. For example, two people are walking down a dark street at night. One is convinced that danger is lurking in every shadow. He is sweating, his heart rate is elevated, his adrenaline levels are abnormally high. The other sees and feels no danger at all. She is relaxed and in an entirely different psychological and physical state, even though the external circumstances are precisely the same.

It's useful to remember that *what* you are thinking is often not as important as *how* you are thinking. Forced, clenched thinking lowers your mood, even if you're thinking "good thoughts." It is the *how* of your thinking that causes your psychological experience. Pressured thought, for example, takes you away from your Insight State of Mind.

Any time you find yourself with a nice feeling or in a great state of mind, notice it. It will remind you of what's natural, and that will support the natural process of returning you to that state. Also, find something to be grateful for. Have you ever thought about how grateful you are for something and then found yourself in a bad mood? It doesn't happen. Gratitude is a mood elevator. When one very successful company president notices that his mood is shot, he walks out of his office and down the hall to find somebody to sincerely thank. He says that he finds such people very easily now. Their mood is lifted, and so is his.

During one of Malcolm's workshops, a participant who had only just been introduced to the Insight State of Mind shared that for years he had noticed a shift in the quality of his thinking immediately after going for a run. He often had great insights into his business and even began to carry a notepad and miniature pen on his morning jogs, but before this conversation he never had the vocabulary to describe the phenomenon or the recognition that his state of mind was facilitating the insights.

Focusing hard on thinking better may work on occasion, but by and large, trying to out-think your thinking is a pretty weak strategy. Techniques can sometimes be helpful, but they will generally get you only so far. And remember, techniques aren't ultimately required. Nothing is. You don't have to *do* anything to alter your state of mind. It doesn't work that way. Changes of mood can accompany action, but they are not caused by action.

> You don't have to *do* anything to alter your state of mind.

Losing awareness of your state of mind is a natural and common occurrence. Think of it as a parallel to the formation of chronic muscular stress. First you tense the muscles. Then you keep the tension. Then a habit of tension is formed. Your brain knows the presence of that muscle only through sensation, so without movement, the sensation extinguishes over time and the brain "loses track" that the now permanently stressed muscle is in fact stressed. After that, nothing changes. The stress is "forgotten." Certain forms of physical therapy and exercise are based simply in restoring movement to tight muscles, thus restoring sensation. With sensation and awareness, the proper mind-body connection is reestablished.

Analogously, what you are looking for is simply awareness and understanding: awareness of your psychological experience moment by moment and deeper and deeper understanding of how your thinking forms your psychological reality—nothing more. *You need only have insights into the nature of your thinking and how your thought creates the world you live in.*

Eventually, you will realize that in any moment you are just one thought away from an insight, one thought away from psychological freedom under any circumstance. This doesn't mean that you can order up that thought on demand. In fact, you probably can't. It means that you know how through your own insights (and this is important), any psychological state is impermanent and not a direct consequence of the situation you are in. Anyone can tell you this. But you must see so for yourself. Your truth is in your own insights into how your thoughts bring about your reality. When you come to see how this relationship works for yourself, you will be forever free from the chronic grip of insecurity or the encumbrance of other low-quality psychological states.

Bad states of mind will become much like storms. Yes, the rain may be coming down quite heavily now, but you know the storm will blow through. You may not be able to do anything to accelerate that process, but you know this simple, powerful truth: it will ultimately pass. This truth allows you to endure the rain with relative equanimity. You permit the natural restorative mental processes to work. The basketball floats. The snow settles. And you don't interfere with these processes by getting bothered or worried or otherwise stressing yourself to get to some place where you would otherwise be if you simply stopped thinking your way out of it.

For a rare few of us, this awareness happens in an éclat of a transformative epiphany. For the rest, it arrives through insights over time—some small and others big. Your understanding will change and deepen. What you know today is different from what you knew about this five years ago, and it will likely be materially different five years from now. Undoubtedly, perhaps even ironically, we may well be thinking and saying different things about insight five years hence.

Whether in the form of minor insights or major epiphanies, your understanding of how we all see the world through the lens of thought will deepen over time. As your appreciation and awareness grow, so will your capacity for insight. Your usual mental hang-ups will shorten, and your ability to rebound from poor thinking will expand. In short, you will operate as a more intuitive, imaginative, and effective thinker.

Remember,

- Only your thinking can take you out of an Insight State of Mind. The outside world is never the culprit.

- Focusing hard on thinking better may work on occasion, but by and large, trying to outthink your mind is not a good idea.

- A genuine awareness of the connection between thought and the reality we perceive will allow a distressed mind to recover quickly and inhabit an Insight State of Mind with greater regularity.

5 Insight in Practice

In *The Art of Thought*, Graham Wallas presented one of the first models of the creative process. It consists of four steps:

Preparation: where the mind focuses on the problem and explores its dimensions

Incubation: where the problem is internalized into the unconscious mind and nothing appears to be happening externally

Illumination/insight: where the creative idea bursts forth from its preconscious processing into conscious awareness

Verification: where the idea is consciously verified, elaborated, and then applied[1]

Fresh thoughts and memory thoughts can be found in each of these steps. Fresh and memory thoughts, learning and recall, and intuition and analysis are all employed in various combinations. We take in information and put it onto mental shelves.

As new information arrives, our brains search to see whether the information we've just taken in is similar to other information already stored on those shelves and, if so, "tags" it as similar. If our brains find a match, the old memories come off the shelf and combine with the new information, resulting in a new thought. Even the most analytical calculation requires judgment and sometimes intuition to recall the appropriate rules, formula, or logic so that it can be applied to the problem at hand. And as we saw with Linus Pauling, in chapter 1, our intuition needs to be fed with material from memory.

More often than not, the pieces and patterns of information are so familiar and come off the shelves so easily that we don't notice these thought processes occurring. However, when a new pattern is formed by a combination of different pieces in a new way, we experience the result as an insight—the famous "aha!"

While scientists have made significant advances in understanding these phenomena, in this chapter we want to focus not on what the neurons are doing but on how to generate more insights. We can use Wallas's model as a map for this. While it appears that the steps are to be taken in sequential order, we will see that, in practice, these steps often blend together.

Framing the Problem

You are already thinking about the problem, so you have "framed" it in a certain way. Framing is easy; your mind does it for you automatically. Reframing is what poses the challenge. Frames are pretty sturdy and get sturdier the more they are reused. So, if you want to think about the problem differently, you can really benefit from an outside perspective, ideally from someone with similar experience with Insight Thinking and without much knowledge about the actual problem.

Imagine for a moment that you have a problem that has been around for a while, and you are confident that you have all the relevant information you need to solve it. (This is usually a generous assumption and something we will return to later.) You might think of yourself as working through the following steps with your partner, but don't get tightly wedded to the steps.

Preparation

Start as you did in the chapter 3 listening exercises, with answering these questions with your partner:

- What is an insight?

- What does your Insight State of Mind feel like?

Once again, this will point your thinking in the right direction—the unknown—and remind you of the most fertile state of mind for insights.

DESIRE

Instead of starting with the problem, begin by describing what you want. What is your desired state of affairs? If the problem ceased to exist, what would the world look like?

These questions begin to flip your perspective and ask what would exist if the problem were no more.

CURRENT REALITY

Using memory thinking, take inventory: What do you know about this problem? What don't you know about this problem?

Then go on a coached Fresh Thought Hunt (chapter 3). What are some fresh thoughts? What else do you know and not know about this problem?

WHAT'S MISSING?

Have your partner coach you on a Fresh Thought Hunt about what's missing from your understanding of the current reality.

People often realize in retrospect that one tiny, missed element changed their ability to see a solution. What's interesting is that the particular piece was always there to be seen; it was just overlooked. So, build out the inventory of your current reality, and see what, if anything, you have missed. Do not bear down hard during this search; maintain an Insight State of Mind.

> People often realize in retrospect that one tiny, missed element changed their ability to see a solution.

It's common for significant insight to occur in the course of these conversations, and it is not unusual for a solution to be discovered. And if not, you have really set the stage for the next step.

Reframing

Go on a Fresh Thought Hunt together focusing on the following questions: How can we look at this problem differently?

What's a new way that we can look at this problem? Describe the problem in as many different, novel ways as you can. Of course, these are classic, creative problem-solving questions. The difference is how we are using them. We are deliberately looking for fresh thoughts and the Insight State of Mind.

You can also try appreciating the problem as it stands: What is good about this issue? Turn your situation into an asset: If this issue is going to persist, then how can you make it a good thing?

For each of these questions, set aside anywhere from five to fifteen minutes—or more if you want. Each will offer different lenses through which to see the world and will disrupt the current thinking. These questions will lead toward higher-quality thought. They shepherd us on the road to a fresh, open state of mind. Eventually, with your new frame of reference, an insight will surface.

Reflection and Incubation

Don't keep pressing through. Often, you need to get away from the problem for a while. Just working on something else for a bit may help, but occasionally a conversation or meeting should be stopped altogether if it has lost focus and is feeling forced. Breaking away is helpful for some but absolutely crucial for others. If you have the time (or even if you don't), sleep on it, go for a walk, or switch tasks. This will help let your mind wander while maintaining your equanimity. Focus not so much on the problem but rather on what you really want. What can you do to get where you want to be? What action could you take right now with the means immediately at your disposal?

People frequently describe how, for the longest time, they were asking the wrong questions, and when they finally asked the right question, the solution appeared right in front of them. This reframing of questions is an excellent focus for this preparation conversation.

Insight

Insight isn't really a separate step. You will likely have had a number of insights during either your preparation or reflection and incubation work. If the solution has not yet occurred to you, return to some of the activities in either of those two steps. Use your good-feeling barometer as a guide in choosing which activities to undertake.

Once you have allowed all your initial work to settle in and given yourself some space to ruminate, it's time to actively search for some insights. Start by reporting any insights you may have had or anything that may have occurred as a result of the actions that you have taken thus far. Next, go on a Fresh Thought Hunt, as described in chapter 3. Make sure that during this step, you avoid the use of your analytical mind. Speak only when you have a fresh thought, and wait patiently with an open mind until one arrives.

Verification

If you settle on a solution to your problem, be sure to verify it with your analytical mind. By reengaging the analytical mind after producing so many fresh thoughts, you will have all sorts of new material to work with and a completely new perspective from which to approach it.

Reminder: What to Look and Listen For

Of course, by now, you will remember to pay close attention to the feeling of each of these conversations and that the only consistent barometer for an Insight State of Mind is indeed its feeling. Remember also to look for fresh thoughts and insights and avoid thoughts from memory. From time to time, pause, reflect, and perhaps even ask your unconscious mind for a fresh thought, and then wait quietly and see what pops into your head.

Following are a few other items that can serve as points of focus, things to be on the lookout for not only with others but in your personal practice as well.

INCONSISTENCIES IN THOUGHT, MISTAKES, ERRORS, AND INACCURACIES

It's common and even desirable to uncover inconsistencies in how you or a colleague is thinking about a particular subject. Sometimes, for example, we find missing pieces or holes in our logic and reasoning. Other times, we may discover contradictions in our interpretation or analysis. You may notice an undifferentiated funny feeling before you can even put something into words. Be sure to explore such feelings.

These inconsistencies and missing pieces are all enormously beneficial because they open up the possibility of new learning and fresh thinking. When uncovered and pointed out by others, a moment of embarrassment or awkwardness almost always arises that we naturally seek to avoid. Regret or disappointment, however, is of no use, and handling such moments adroitly and with compassion can open major doors into insight. This particular skill can be learned, but it does take practice. Catching or being caught in a case of some flawed thinking often provokes defensive feelings and behaviors. While seemingly counterintuitive at first, these moments should be celebrated. You want to move through these embarrassing or defensive feelings as quickly as you can. Luckily, the more you habitually look for the good feeling in your state of mind, the more quickly you will recover when discovering inconsistencies or flaws in your thinking and the less you will engender embarrassment when you happen to spot it in others. You will find that as your resilience in these moments grows, so will the resilience of those around you.

THINGS YOU DON'T KNOW

Park the things you think you know and look for things you don't. Unanswered questions keep your thinking pointed toward the unknown, where, by definition, you will find insight. Taking stock of what you don't know, from time to time, allows you to identify these questions and jump off on new paths of exploration.

NEW QUESTIONS OR TOPICS YOU WOULD LIKE AN INSIGHT INTO

New questions will often occur to you while you are listening. Be sure to make a note of them. Review the facts and ask yourself, "What question hasn't been asked or demands asking?" Question a particular fact. Is it true, and if so, how can you be sure? What would be a useful topic to have an insight on at this particular time?

ASSUMPTIONS

Occasionally inventory and challenge the basic assumptions you have about the issue. Reflect on what you think is true. If it's true, how can you be sure? Could it be otherwise?

The above is nowhere near a complete list of what to look and listen for, but it is a good starting point. Be sure you are looking toward that feeling of wonder and curiosity. Of course, these questions and processes are well known. It's the state of mind that makes them conducive to insight.

Working with Others Is Powerful

Hunting for insights with more than one person is particularly effective. Fresh thought from multiple perspectives can help free us when we have become too familiar with an issue.

EXERCISE:

Working as a Trio

OVERVIEW

One of the most popular exercises we use with our clients involves two people helping a third have insights into a problem or topic of interest. This is not unlike the Insight Listening exercise from chapter 3 with one other person, except that you will have twice the minds on the job and a very different overall dynamic. An illustration can be found on our website, TAOI Online Learning.

Find two people who are interested in helping you have an insight on a particular issue. While preferable, it is not necessary that the participants have knowledge or training in Insight Thinking. You may be surprised to learn that it is generally better if the two people do not know much about the topic that you are bringing to the table.

Begin by describing what an insight is to you and what your Insight State of Mind feels like. All the three participants should engage in this conversation, trying to speak with fresh thoughts and staying in a quiet mind. Don't describe a moment of insight that you have thought about dozens of times before. Do mention any thought that feels new and fresh.

THE EXERCISE

There are two roles (one speaker and two listeners). Have one of the listeners monitor the time, or set an alarm using a watch or phone.

Part 1

The speaker describes his issue in sixty seconds or less while the other two people listen quietly. They should remain completely silent and refrain from asking any questions. For part 1 of this exercise, the listeners face their chairs toward the speaker, as shown in figure 1.

Part 2

Once the sixty seconds is up or the speaker has finished (whichever comes first), the listeners should swivel their

Figure 1 Listeners face speaker

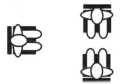

Figure 2 Listeners face each other

chairs to face each other (preferably with the speaker out of their line of sight) as shown in figure 2.

The listeners in this part should be looking for a good feeling, not barking out the first thought that comes to mind. In fact, the period allotted for sharing fresh thoughts begins in a silence that lasts until a light bulb flashes for one of the participants.

Now, begin to reflect on the topic that was just described. Similar to the two-person exercise from chapter 3, the purpose here is to spend five minutes sharing only fresh thoughts on the subject. Each time either listener has a truly fresh thought on the subject, she shares it with the other listener while being "overheard" by the speaker.

Remember that the purpose is neither to solve the problem nor to give advice, both of which will bring everyone back to memory thinking. It is rather to generate fresh thought around the subject and help facilitate an insight in the speaker. If a memory thought must be spoken to get it out of the way, identify it as you speak it, and then move back into fresh thoughts.

The speaker, throughout this part of the exercise, sits aside. His instinct will be to analyze, correct, or dismiss what the others are saying, but instead, the speaker must remain quiet and look for fresh thoughts and insights, perhaps jotting down on a notepad the thoughts that seem particularly fresh.

The speaker must be careful not to judge the listeners based on their lack of knowledge or experience in the subject. People with a lifetime of relevant experience often have profound insights into their business based on a simple remark from someone in a completely unrelated field of expertise.

Part 3

After the listeners have spent five minutes sharing their fresh thoughts on the subject, the speaker may step back into the mix and comment on the experience.

The speaker should now take two minutes or less to report any new insights that may have occurred during the exercise and comment on what it was like listening to the others discuss the topic using only fresh thinking.

After the speaker has described his experience, the listeners should join the conversation and describe what the experience was like for them. In this last part, everyone should continue to speak only from fresh thoughts and avoid giving advice, and the speaker should talk only around 10 percent of the time. The tendency will be for the speaker to talk as much if not more than the two listeners, but this should be avoided to get the best value from the exercise.

The three parts form one complete round of the trio exercise. If you like, at this point you can switch the role of speaker and repeat the exercise using a new topic.

KEEP IN MIND

This exercise works wonderfully when people follow the structure closely. By offering a very brief description of the problem (perhaps even in thirty seconds instead of sixty) and then stepping aside, the speaker should be able to remove himself from a setting where in most cases he would be inclined to hijack the discussion. When we hear people talking about something that we have a stake in or consider personal, our tendency is to jump in and correct the line of thinking by guiding it back toward the direction we originally had in mind. As soon as we start leading the conversation, listeners are inclined to follow and the result is that everyone gets on the same page, curtailing the likelihood of anything fresh!

Charlie's Trio Story

Here is an example of an exercise that Charlie recently partici-pated in with a couple of clients.

> I had a group of executives participating in this trio exercise, and I decided to join in as the third member of one of the groups. Lately, I had been dealing with a project I had been working on with a number of other people. At the time, it seemed to me that a good number of them were simply not doing their jobs. The result was that I ended up having to step in and pull things together so that everything that needed to get done would get done. I was in a low mood about the whole situation, and it looked like it was going to be hours of more work for me.
>
> I explained this in thirty seconds to my two partners. They turned toward each other, and right away I knew that they got it. They are managers, so they know what it's like when the people who are supposed to be doing their work aren't doing it. But almost imme-diately, they began to get off track and started talking about moving houses and whose job it is to unpack after a move, the husband's or the wife's.
>
> I was doing my very best to drop the one thought that was continually coming back into my head: "There's no relationship whatsoever between their discussion and my problem." A moment later I thought, "They're not talking about my problem at all." I wasn't getting riled up about the fact that what they were saying

wasn't relevant; in fact, I was in a relatively good state of mind because that was one of the guidelines I had set up, and I wanted to be a quality participant in the exercise. Then I thought, "Whatever they're talking about, it's not my problem!" And all of a sudden it hit me like the proverbial ton of bricks: "*This isn't my problem.* It's not my problem; it's the project leader's problem. And it's *her* job. She's just not doing it."

My problem had vanished. All I had to do for it to completely disappear was to write an e-mail that pleasantly said, "These things aren't getting done, and they are your job, not mine." It was absolutely magnificent. The issue disappeared even before the e-mail was written—gone in the space of a thought. And of course, the truth of the matter was that I was the one who needed to be reminded even more than my colleagues on the project.

Allison's Story

Allison Zmuda is an education consultant and friend who describes her experience of this process in her book *Breaking Free from Myths about Teaching and Learning.*

At a workshop I attended, the facilitators instructed us to engage two other people in a conversation about a problem we cared deeply about and had devoted much time to solving but that still had us stuck. The only rule was that no one was allowed to say anything aloud that they had already thought of before:

no familiar anecdotes or analogies, and no repetition of all the reasons why it couldn't be done. It was the most awkward conversation that I have ever engaged in, but one of the most fascinating. Every time I started to open my mouth, I would close it again, self-censoring according to the rule. After a dozen of these false starts, I began to realize that I had become pretty boring to listen to. Forget about how I came off to family, friends, and colleagues, I had become boring to myself. I had grown comfortable with the notion that any new problem was a familiar problem that I likely either had the answer to or had some authority to speak on and had become increasingly uninterested in the power of context, perception, and new connections. My brain may be designed to look for a memory-based answer to a question, but it also has the capacity for something more.

While developing the capacity to think deeply and create new connections requires practice, the possibility is always there, waiting for you. Simply calling attention to the ability to do so improves the quality of a learning experience. Let's go back to the conversation with the serious problem and the rule that had rendered me mute.

I found that once I gave up searching for answers to my problem and started listening to the conversation about it, I became engaged not with the dialogue in my head, but with the thoughts shared by these two people. As the content and feeling behind their words penetrated, I began to see new connections, and finally, seven minutes into the conversation, I had something to say. It wasn't long and it wasn't pithy, but it had integrity and originality.

The brain can be trained in how to respond to life. When thought settles down and an individual experiences a reprieve from operating in hyper-drive, insights become possible. Some individuals experience this reprieve through running, others through knitting, others through watching tides ebb and flow, but it is possible for anyone to create space that allows for creativity, wisdom, and insight to arrive.[2]

Insight and Problems

Probably the most common time that we want an insight is when we have a problem and need a solution. Most of us have had an insight that solves a problem, and then our very next thought is about why we didn't think of it earlier. If you look closely, implicit in this statement is that the solution was there for some time, but you just didn't see it. Since the solution was available the whole time, your problem wasn't really the problem. The problem was that you simply couldn't see the solution.

Where did the problem go after it was solved?

We have touched on this before, but consider this: where did the problem go after it was solved? Often it dissolves in an instant, and in some cases, you can't remember what it was, even if you try. How can something that has been present for a week, a month, a year, or ten years be real if it can also just cease to exist? Where did it go? Something that vanishes so completely and so instantaneously can't have been that (physically) real in the first place.

Alone

So far in this chapter, we have assumed that you have access to someone who can help you open up your thinking. Other approaches that you are familiar with may be equally helpful if they are in the spirit of Insight Thinking and if you avoid advice giving. The key is to get yourself out of an entrenched way of thinking, which can be tricky when you are left to your own mental devices. This is perhaps the main reason why it's so useful to have others around to assist you on this journey.

If you don't have anyone to help you or if you prefer working on your own, here are a few ideas that may be helpful. If you generally have insights when you are by yourself, then you probably have your own process for generating fresh ideas, and if it works, you should use it. If that process is stale, however, or if you find yourself alone and in need of some fresh thinking, try some of these tips:

- *Change your physical setting.* Change your environment, ideally to one that you find encourages a quiet mind. Try going for a walk, taking a nap, or listening to some music.

- *Set the problem entirely aside, and instead reflect on this question: What can I do right now to make it more likely that I might have an insight?* Ask yourself for a fresh thought about something you could do differently that might open up a new thought. The new thought can be about anything. It will be beneficial even if it doesn't reference the original problem. Said another way, this technique directs you to look for an insight about having insights but not only about the current problem. If you come up with an answer that feels good, execute it, and then see what happens.

- *Use a pen and paper as a stand-in for another person.* Note taking with an Insight State of Mind can be a powerful activity. You might even create a written dialogue. This can help objectify your thinking.

Any conversation and most any problem-solving technique can be enhanced with Insight Thinking. First and foremost, maintain an Insight State of Mind and look for fresh thoughts. When you are working with someone else, don't get caught up in his or her problem, and don't offer advice. If you lose the good feeling or if you encounter a spate of thoughts that feel tired or stale, switch gears and look for fresh thoughts and insights. Always remember to verify your insights with critical thinking before acting whenever possible.

Most of our issues in life are products of our thinking and thus completely dissolve with the right insight. As you practice TAOI, you will find that fresh thought, intuition, memory thought, and analysis all work together without your conscious attention, and only when a new pattern is formed in a new way will you experience a substantive aha moment.

6 The Art of Insight in Organizations

Anything we've discussed in previous chapters can easily be put to use at the office. Now we are going to focus specifically on teams and larger groups. TAOI can be added to virtually any existing organization process or procedure with great benefit since few things don't benefit from looking and listening for insight and a good feeling. Sometimes it's best to lace an existing procedure with short applications of these methods. Other times it might make sense to completely revise a procedure and base it on insight.

Our aim in this chapter is to give you a few examples to spark your imagination and leave it to you to figure out the best way to apply these methods in your situation. We are going to recount a number of stories from the various settings where we have employed TAOI. Some of the applications may seem too big a leap at first, and generally it's not a good idea, nor is it necessary, to replace existing processes until you have some experience.

Meetings

The Art of Insight can be applied in all sorts of meetings in the normal course of business. What you should look to do is

- Use TAOI and a Fresh Thought Hunt to plan how you might use the method in advance of a meeting and incorporate it into your design
- Use TAOI spontaneously, either throughout the entire meeting or intermittently

Staff Meetings

Here is one manager's description of the difference in his monthly staff meetings after applying TAOI:

> We have about five people in the room and another five on a conference line for this five-hour meeting that starts at lunch and runs until the end of the day. In the past, we would march through the agenda according to our rules for good meeting management. We'd grind away at each topic according to schedule and arrive exhausted at the end. Incredibly, we were accustomed to wasting huge amounts of time in our meetings.
>
> Now we manage this meeting much more effectively. When I recognize the meeting is off track or we're spinning in a circle or feeling bad, I stop it. Sometimes I call a break, or other times we just move on to something else and come back to the sticky issue later. In fact, I find myself adjusting the agenda to make sure

the stuff I think is going to be a bit of a grind goes toward the end. That allows us to do as much as we can when we're fresh and stop when we realize we need to stop. We see a huge increase in productivity from this shift. The ability to refocus on other important things when you know you're getting nowhere on a particular subject has been very valuable.

We have many successful examples of this style of meeting. One head of a research and development function who was known for her hard-driving style found herself once again aggressively driving a two-day meeting of twenty or so of her assembled global leaders. It was getting nowhere, and at about two thirty in the afternoon, much to everyone's astonishment, she called a halt to the meeting for the day, telling people that they were still "in" her meeting and had to follow her instructions. They should go on a break for the rest of the day (not go back to their desks or e-mail, etc.) and enjoy each other's company. They should talk informally about the important business and technical issues they had identified and generate new perspectives and insights and return the next day prepared to share them.

You know where this is going. They started the next morning with people sharing their realizations. Enormous progress was made, and numerous participants reported that it was the single best meeting in their careers with the company.

The Offsite Planning Session

Here's a situation that was completely driven by insight—an annual planning meeting. Our colleague Joel Yanowitz was asked to facilitate a small firm's annual planning retreat. As is common in these situations, he had some preparatory meetings with the executive team and interviews with a few other members of the eighteen people who would be present. Based on these meetings, and with the president's consent, Joel began the three-day offsite with a simple question:

> Well, you all know how these things go, don't you? You've each got a few issues that you think the company desperately needs to address. Normally, we would fill two or three flip charts with these questions or issues and then somehow prioritize them, assign times, and march ourselves through each of them in sequence, managing ourselves to stay within the time allotted for each section. We would carefully record the follow-up tasks and accountabilities. And then do some sort of critique at the end of the three days. If we are lucky, everyone will report how great the meeting was and how much we got accomplished. Does that sound familiar?

People nodded yes and Joel posed another question: "Are you all excited and really looking forward to this?"

Everyone admitted no. It was hard to be truly excited about three days of slogging through a list of problems and issues with the prospect that success would mean long to-do lists for everyone in the room, each of whom already had a very full plate.

At this point, Joel said, "Let's try something different." He described a little bit about fresh thoughts and The Art of Insight and finished with an invitation:

Here's the process: We take a couple of minutes to see if there are any other issues that need to go up here on our list. Then we look over this list and pick the one that feels most intuitively right and begin there. We'll take as much time as feels good to spend on that issue. Then we'll see which issue speaks to us the most next and tackle that one. And so on. And here's the deal. You'll be looking for insights and fresh thoughts and trying to stay in a good state of mind. I'll be a sentinel for the mood within the room, and if it feels like things get thick or we lose a good feeling, I'll call a break. Let's try it for an hour or two. It can't hurt, and you probably will find that you really like it. Want to give it a go?

This was an intrepid group, so they quickly agreed. They worked on the first task and after about an hour felt really good about having had a couple of insights into this first issue. They took a break and then moved on to what they chose as the next most attractive issue, following the same process. By the end of the morning, they were only on the third issue of a list of about twenty, but the insights that emerged led to very different and unexpected actions. They decided to continue the process after lunch, and by the end of the afternoon they had discussed perhaps five of the proposed issues, each time selecting the next issue to focus on based on the intuition in the room. The feeling of progress was so strong that even though they had made "less than normal progress" in terms of an agenda, they broke at about four thirty, had cocktails and dinner, socialized in the evening, and planned to continue in the same mode the next day.

The following morning, people shared any overnight insights that they had, which precipitated an hour-long discussion and a wealth of fresh thoughts. Then they launched into the next issue, continuing in this mode through the rest of the morning and into the early afternoon, when something surprising occurred. The group was working on the tenth issue, and as they brought it to a nice conclusion and then looked to see what was left, they realized that in the course of addressing their first ten issues, all the other issues had either been discussed and resolved or had been rendered irrelevant. They were essentially done by about two thirty on the second day of a three-day meeting! Wisely, they declared success, broke early, and had a great social time together for the rest of that day. They reconvened the next morning (they had paid for the hotel rooms, after all) and covered a few housekeeping tasks, and everyone went home early completely excited.

Of course, not every meeting will turn out like this one, but nevertheless, this example gives you a sense of what can happen with the spontaneous application of The Art of Insight and a well-intentioned group.

Solving Problems, Particularly Intractable Ones

We have found that The Art of Insight can be particularly helpful when a problem has been around for a long time and has resisted multiple solutions. In many cases, all that needs to be known about the issue is in fact already known within the firm, but the pieces haven't been assembled properly. The solution would not likely be found in further study or analysis. An insight—a new view of the problem—is what is needed. Of course, this is often true of other problems firms face, so you don't have to limit the use of TAOI to intransigent issues.

> The solution would not likely be found in further study or analysis.

When we help clients use TAOI to solve problems, we aim to forestall the normal tendency to push to a solution or closure. Instead, we want people to discipline themselves to keep looking into the unknown for what they haven't seen already, allowing fresh thoughts and insights to occur until one of them takes hold and captures their attention and imagination. Each subsequent step along the way is not based on a previous design but is instead guided by fresh thinking in that moment about what would be the right thing to do next.

Here's what happened with a division of a global food company. After three years of struggle, it was pretty clear that the company's strategy for entry into Chinese markets and using China for global production was failing. A team of eight was assembled from around the world for a three-day meeting to address the problem. Each member came equipped with his or her own diverse and deep experience but without any preparation other than reading the currently existing analyses and reports.

After being given some background on TAOI, the team reconfirmed their vision for what they wanted their China business to look like and began to explore the current reality and what they had learned. Instead of trying to convince each other of the validity of their personal, previously found conclusions, they limited their conversations to what they thought they knew were facts and fresh thoughts. Each person described what he or she thought the problem was, and—no surprise— each saw it differently to some significant degree. The team began to look for more novel problem descriptions.

After about ninety minutes, they took stock of what they had discussed. What points was there general agreement on? (Recognizing that there is always a risk of "groupthinking" something that in fact isn't true, these were set aside for the time being.) On which points were there disagreements? Of this group, those that could best be answered through analysis were also set aside for later. The team took a break, and when they returned, they focused their attention on two areas. The first involved the remaining disagreements that they felt would be best addressed through fresh thoughts and insights. What would explain the differences in perception? Could a different lens or perspective resolve the conflict—a different characterization of the problem? The second area involved what they didn't know that somehow seemed important to know.

As the explorations and discussions deepened, more and different understandings of reality began to emerge. The team had a couple of flip charts filled with new statements of the problem. After a few hours, reality began to settle in. The business needed a product with a certain water content, and each attempt at at-scale manufacturing had failed on quality and total cost of delivery. Then in the next moment, they saw the problem would be easy to fix. The technical problem was substantial, but the engineering representative said that it was solvable if it could be made a priority and his engineers could stop chasing some of the nearly thirty other projects that were on their wish list and the wish lists of their sister divisions. There was a manufacturing issue, but that one had actually been solved when a new plant was started in Indiana a few months earlier. In just a few minutes, the team recognized that the solution was easily within the company's grasp.

Then a second insight hit. Yes, they had framed the problem, which showed them a solution that was obvious in retrospect. At the same time, it showed them a problem in virtually all their other businesses. They were providing specialty technical support to commodity customers and consequently were unnecessarily overservicing virtually everyone at great cost.

This gave way to concern that the solutions were so simple that the executive board that had sponsored the initiative would not support them. They spent the remainder of the three days looking for holes below the water line—anything that could show a flaw in their reasoning. None were found, and the team took the plan to the board while simultaneously gently socializing it with a few people within the functions of the company who would be responsible for implementation. The board found the solution spectacular in its simplicity and effectiveness, as did the future functional owners. The groundswell of support led to the creation of a Design-for-Six-Sigma project that ultimately implemented the solution.

How Is Insight Different from Problem Solving?

As Robert Fritz observed in his book *Creating*, the aim of creating is to bring something into existence, and the object of problem solving is often to drive something—the problem—out of existence.[1] TAOI is essentially a creative act, an act that starts in the unknown and results in something that is known, perhaps in an unimaginably deep way. Problem solving, while ideally precipitating novel and previously unseen solutions, is more like playing with a jigsaw puzzle, where you assemble already-known pieces. You are pleased when all the pieces finally fit. With an insight, however, you are sometimes blown away.

TAOI complements any of the better-known problem-solving methods. An obvious use is during the "divergent" phase that aims to get lots of possible solutions on the table. Less obvious, but perhaps more valuable, is during the "convergent" phase, which often resembles that jigsaw puzzle where the previously identified possibilities are sifted, analyzed, and tested to arrive at the final proposal. It's here that you can really benefit from the ongoing and deliberate search for fresh thoughts and insights.

> TAOI complements any of the better-known problem-solving methods.

The TAOI-oriented session is aimed at having an insight rather than setting up a number of solutions for subsequent analysis. Divergence occurs, but it is not that structured, and convergence occurs when the insight hits. There really isn't a separate phase.

How The Art of Insight Differs from Brainstorming

In one organization, people were well trained on building on the ideas of others—to the point that this was the norm and, indeed, an overused strategy. This led to wildly fast-paced meetings where numerous but rarely fresh ideas tumbled all over the place. Kay, a relatively senior organization member and the only person who had experience with TAOI, had been listening quietly in a meeting when she finally broke into the conversation. She was about five words into her sentence when she stopped cold. There was a pause, and the room went silent because of the trained respect that people had developed for each other when sharing ideas. Then Kay said, "You know, that's not going to be a fresh thought." She said no more and handed her "turn" to whoever was going to jump in next. The room stayed silent for several seconds. Then somebody spoke, starting with, "Well, here *is* a fresh one." A couple more fresh thoughts tumbled out after that, with various other people reinforcing, perhaps unconsciously, the difference between them and the already-stated ideas that usually made up their discussions.

When the session is properly staged, a team employing Insight Thinking will behave quite differently than if they were brainstorming. Brainstorms are typically very fast paced without pauses, and Insight Thinking is comparatively slow with many pauses, aims for a reflective mood, and always looks to maintain a good feeling. In brainstorming, no particular censoring of memory thoughts occurs. In Insight Thinking, old thoughts are discouraged. The two modes are different and yet wonderfully complementary, and if you switch back and forth between the two, you will probably find your brainstorming mode getting quieter and more reflective.

Strategy Formulation

There are probably as many strategy methodologies out there as there are strategy consultants. These approaches are generally meant to be scientific and rely heavily on analytics. To overgeneralize a bit, they usually begin by creating a host of strategic options, and then, by applying sophisticated mathematical and analytic procedures, they determine the means, cost, and economic value of the options. Once the optimal strategy is selected, it then becomes a matter of implementing that strategy. Product lines and other assets are sold and acquired. Reorganization occurs, and occasionally attempts at cultural change are made. Once all these steps are successful, the company defends the new strategic high ground for the next several years until the strategy wears thin and must once again be revised through a similar process.

Various assaults on the intellectual soundness of this approach have been made over the past few years, but nevertheless, it remains a prevalent framework and has many opportunities to integrate The Art of Insight. One particularly worthwhile place is where the process includes the establishment of a mission or vision. This sort of undertaking can benefit profoundly from the deep, creative discussions that grow out of fresh thinking.

Here is an example of what can happen when a strategy is based on an insight. Early in 1977, Dick Kovacevich was made head of the New York Banking Division at Citicorp. At the time, the group was losing $100 million a year, despite having one-third of the market. Like any smart executive joining a new organization, Dick engaged his leaders in numerous conversations to find out where the business had gone wrong and how best to correct it. As he probed, he discovered that the market was being defined exclusively as personal checking accounts. Not only was this wrong in his mind, but as defined, Citi's market share was already so high that the profit problem was virtually unsolvable. Then he had an insight. If the market were defined more broadly to include other financial products and services that consumers routinely purchased, Citi's share would become 3 percent with enormous possibility for growth. Then he had an even bigger insight. Most of Citi's customers were already purchasing these products and services some-where—it just wasn't from Citi!

The new strategy was simple and common sense: get these existing customers to bring to Citi the business they were already giving to others. It was obvious that it could work, and if it did, it would be successful for at least five years. No substantive forecast or studies were performed. Instead, the division members just went out in some of the branches and tried selling current customers additional products. It not only worked immediately, but the division quickly realized that the cost of selling a new product to an existing customer was one-tenth that of selling the same product to a new customer. When Dick was promoted three years later, Citi's share had grown to 11 percent with annual profits in excess of $100 million.

Reading this story, you might find yourself questioning whether this is an example of a great insight or it is just an example of a good leader coming in with some common sense. After all, this is the sort of thing that good banks do. But this is exactly the point. *After the insight, it just looks like common sense!* If this strategy was so obvious, then why hadn't it already happened in Citi's previous one hundred years of successful retail banking? In the late 1970s, the strategy was revolutionary. In fact, even today's banks across the world still struggle to do it well.

The story doesn't end there. In 1986, Dick joined Norwest Bank, ultimately becoming its CEO. At the time, Norwest was a small regional bank on the brink of failure, experiencing fierce competition from the big national banks that benefited from size and cost advantages. Norwest was struggling with how to differentiate itself in a way that would allow it to thrive. Based on his experience at Citi, Dick had complete confidence in what he termed *integrated cross-selling*.

Dick observed to us, "Once you have the insight, it's really all in the execution. But make no mistake, that's a lot of work." In his first ninety days at Norwest, Dick, with other members of his executive team, visited practically all of Norwest's 273 branches, holding town-hall-style meetings to educate everyone about integrated cross-selling. During the course of these meetings, the team had another insight. Norwest should be able to provide large bank products and services to small bank customers and do it more personally than any of the national banks. They could "out-local the nationals and out-national the locals."

Using "out-local the nationals" and integrated cross-selling, Norwest flourished and, over the years, purchased and merged with other banks, including Wachovia and Wells Fargo, whose name it retained. What started as a small regional agricultural bank worth less than $1 billion, now has a market value of $190 billion, making it, with the exception of two banks partially owned by the Chinese government, the most valuable financial institution in the entire world. Over the past twenty-five years, the insight-based retail banking strategy has remained essentially unchanged and has been applied to commercial banking and other financial services.

TAOI is often used as part of a group process (like the China project). Other times executives have largely developed the strategy themselves out of conversations with colleagues. One executive, Terry Ann, was dealing with the recognition that her company's current strategy was not scalable:

> About a year ago I started developing a new strategic plan in my old style—writing a lot of notes and such. However, a few months ago I decided to just sit back and see what happens. I had a lot of conversations with other staff members about what we really wanted to do and what made us special. Over a short period of time the new plan became clear to me, probably because I haven't been actively doing all that overthinking and overanalyzing I used to do in my attempts to "figure it all out." Instead, it just came together on its own accord.

These stories point to some of the key differences between an insight strategy and a strategy derived from analysis. In the former, you start with the idea and then do *only those analytics necessary to ensure its validity and catch any fatal flaws.* There is no "boiling the ocean" of all the various alternatives. In the case of Norwest, no significant strategy studies have ever been done in the retail banking group. This means far less work, and it means that the formation of strategy is completed quickly, often in as little as three months. Typically, many different people within the organization participate in the formation of a strategy and they often begin acting immediately on their insights. As a consequence, instead of being a second distinct phase, implementation is well underway with momentum building by the time the strategy is formally adopted. In the cases we are familiar with, when insight-based strategies have been used to effect organizational change, the results have never been wrenching, and "cultural change programs" have never been necessary. Norwest never put itself or any of its successors through a forced march to become something different.

We have no way of knowing for sure whether piles of analytics will lead to a better strategy, but when TAOI is employed, participants report that the results are actionable and swiftly implemented.

A multibillion-dollar business probably shouldn't abandon its existing process in favor of searching for "the one game-changing insight." However, TAOI absolutely is something worth testing with one particular product or business unit, as a complement to an existing analytic strategy process, or as a part of a midcourse review of an existing strategy.

If you decide to proceed in this direction, start by having a series of conversations that follow the same format and guidelines we have described earlier. Get your people together and ask questions that take them deeper into their current reality and the unknown, and utilize the many other strategy questions that have been developed by academics and practitioners over the years. Ask them for fresh thoughts on the strategic situation and for their opinions on what makes your organization great. As you have likely noticed by now, the specifics are far less important than the spirit and feeling that accompany this process. Keep talking and searching until an insight hits.

Coaching a Colleague

The Art of Insight can be both exciting and rich when used at work with one other individual. Imagine for a moment that a colleague has come to you for help on a problem. It could be about a technical issue, career guidance, or planning for the next year. The request for help may be deliberate, or it might arise in the normal course of a conversation about something completely different. Let's say you are a good problem solver and the appearance of a problem is like a bucket of raw meat thrown at a lion. You're on it in a heartbeat—looking forward to the physical and psychological pleasure that you will experience when the problem is solved. This time, try something different. Don't try to solve the problem for your colleague. Don't offer advice. Drop immediately into Insight Listening and begin coaching *her* to generate fresh thoughts and unseen but relevant questions as you learned in the Coaching for Fresh Thoughts and Insights exercise.

Keep your mental finger on the feeling of the conversation—stay lighthearted and open. Steer away from premature resolution and help your colleague generate a raft of fresh thoughts. It's likely that she will find an insight or her own solution to the problem. As one manager, Doug, explained,

> Keep your mental finger on the feeling of the conversation—stay lighthearted and open.

When I put this into practice, I'm able to operate from a place where I realize that people have every-thing they need inherently in them. I'm able to just be with them and hear what they have to say. If I am present and quiet enough to allow it, more often than not they will have the insights and discover the solu-tions that they need to move forward.

This approach allows people to discover what they already know without my expecting that they will follow me and accept all my ideas. I feel like I have stepped out of a judgmental mind and have become more of an observer.

Another manager, Dave, described it this way:

As far as insight is concerned, understanding my state of mind is the first thing I notice when I interact with others. In general, I find I'm a lot more calm and centered. I pay much more attention to the conver-sation I'm in, which lets me appreciate both the way it's evolving and the individual statements made. As a result, I also sense in others a greater awareness of the content and meaning of the conversation. I'm simply having different, and better, interactions with people.

Personality Conflict

One particularly nice place to use The Art of Insight is where you find yourself in some sort of persistent conflict with a peer, a subordinate, or even your boss. See if you can engage the other person in looking for some fresh thinking into what the root of the difficulty is. He may not bite on this offer, in which case you can still unilaterally take some of the actions we share below. But for the sake of our illustration, assume that he takes you up on this proposal.

Go on a Fresh Thought Hunt together. Encourage yourself and the other person to look for fresh thoughts. Listen as deeply as you can and, above all, maintain a good feeling. You may not talk 50 percent of the time, but as the conversation progresses, your rapport will deepen. The most important point is to enjoy a good feeling together. The more deeply you listen, the more deeply the other person will experience a connection with you. Even if you do not crack the code on the first meeting, you will feel far better about each other. Your working relationship will improve dramatically. And over time, you will find your conflict abating.

Pete, a senior vice president, found himself constantly arguing with his boss, Charlie (not your author), on nearly everything. Both were disturbed by how difficult their relationship had become given that they had previously been close colleagues. As part of the firm's strategy review process, both were exposed in some depth to The Art of Insight and, in particular, the importance of maintaining a good feeling.

We returned a few months after the strategy review, and as part of our check-in with Pete, we asked him how it was going with Charlie. "Just fine," he said, looking somewhat puzzled that we asked. "Glad to hear that," we responded, "given the problems you guys seemed to be having." Pete was silent for a moment and then said, "I had completely forgotten. We're having a great time together these days. We listen really carefully to each other and are really aware when the feeling of our conversations goes south. The few times it does, we just table the issue and come back to it later. I can't think of a time that we've had an emotional argument in months."

Leading and Facilitating TAOI Discussions

Bringing these new ideas into an organization is best done by the person leading a project or meeting since all teams look to their leader and will roll with almost anything if they see the leader is comfortable with it and thinks it's important. However, you need to be careful about one preexisting condition. If one person on a team is aggressively negative about the idea of using TAOI, the process will probably be difficult if not impossible. Generally, all team members must be at least open-minded about employing this approach, and hopefully you and at least one or two folks will be genuinely enthusiastic.

When using Insight Thinking with a team, you should begin by developing a common language around insight. Start by discussing how to recognize the difference between a fresh thought and a memory thought, and then propose the concept of an Insight State of Mind. Describe your understanding of Insight Thinking and share with your team the importance of their catching on to their own thinking patterns.

Setting the Ground Rules

Once the team members have settled in to the idea of paying attention to their thoughts and they begin to see the value of maintaining an Insight State of Mind, have the group discuss a topic while employing Insight Thinking.

Here are some ground rules that we have found very ef fective:

1. Propose a topic, question, or point of concern. To start, all participants should sit quietly and, as best they can, listen with nothing on their minds. Thoughts are going to arise, but if they are memory thoughts, they should be dropped without giving them voice. You may well experience a long pause at this point. This is a good thing.

2. If a member of the group has a fresh thought relevant to the discussion, that person should share it out loud as soon as convenient while being aware of, but not disrupting, the good feeling of the conversation.

When you run a meeting with these criteria, the pace will slow, and people will become more reflective. A generative and open space will be created, spawning crisp new ideas. Occasionally, running a meeting like this can be somewhat awkward, particularly if some people are left in the dark about what is going on. However, if your team members are well briefed and understand the objective, you shouldn't encounter any problems. If the atmosphere in the room feels free and productive, then you're in good shape.

If things get uncomfortable, however, then some group management may be necessary. The first step is to recognize and announce that the good feeling has been lost. This is pretty easy to do when you are an outside consultant with nothing invested in the content of the conversation. It's more difficult when you are in the thick of matters, but with a modest bit of awareness and practice, it can be learned.

If the loss of the good-feeling state is caught early on, generally only one person needs to mention this before people realize what has happened and then shift back to a good state of mind. On the other hand, if the loss has gone too far or gone on too long, this simple intervention might not be enough. The best step to take at this point is to call a mandatory break. It may well be resisted since the overwhelming inclination in these cases is to power through. A fifteen-minute break is, nevertheless, exactly what is needed. Think of it as a penalty flag that anyone in the group can throw that "stops the game," creating the space and possibility for a break in the thinking and mood. One advantage of working with a group of people familiar with and committed to Insight Thinking is that the more members there are, the more likely someone will catch the loss of mood and throw a flag.

Team members using these ground rules will quickly realize that everything they hear is fresh at least for someone else. In some cases, a new idea may be fresh for every individual in the room, but even if it's new for only a fraction of the group, it will encourage more fresh thoughts for these team members to build on, which can in turn be shared again. The value in laying these ground rules is that the meeting will shed its usual staleness for a more productive and stimulating discussion, where rehashing old thinking is simply not the norm. The tone and feeling of the group will become fresh, and a new energy will permeate the room. Meetings like these entrain people to reach for freshness, get more comfortable with new concepts, and grow less attached to the old ones. Pauses in conversation become more common, and people are allowed to complete their thoughts without interruption. Instead of a person's idea getting hijacked by someone else and steered purposefully in a new direction toward the other person's agenda, the idea has a chance to be consummated in its entirety. It is often remarkable how sure we can be about where an idea may be leading, only to discover that it flows in an entirely different direction. This experience is rich and garners surprise and curiosity. These results are all born from sharing only fresh ideas and listening with nothing on your mind.

You Can Practice TAOI Even for a Few Minutes at a Time

We often run entire meetings using TAOI, but you can carve out just five minutes from a meeting being run in your typical style to shake things up with some Insight Thinking. Particularly if a good number of the team are experienced with Insight Thinking, a five-minute "practice session" will often take the meeting in a new direction, both in terms of the content being discussed and the manner in which it is being discussed.

Take a silent pause for sixty seconds (long enough for a few settling breaths). Then invite people to resume talking when they have a fresh thought. Have a "required" five-second pause between the time one person finishes speaking and the moment the next person starts. This prevents people from getting into a cycle of reacting to whatever the last person said and allows a little time for their thoughts to settle and to notice if something fresh emerges.

Our colleague Joel has been known to encourage people to look out the window whenever they feel like it (assuming there are windows and the view is somewhat pleasant) and let their minds drift a bit with the aim of coming back into the room with some fresh perspective.

Stop for a moment and contrast the setting described above with a typical meeting where the thinking is closed and stagnant and people spend their time restating things that are either obvious or have already been said. You're far less likely to find something new or unusual when you're operating out of memory. Although you have a different set of facts than each person in the room, it's not the content that precipitates an insight. Occasionally, a new piece of data will trigger a new idea, but much more reliably, a state of mind is what sparks an insight because we are finally noticing something different in the available facts. The continuous repetition of content that has already been stated may be an efficient way to win an argument, but it is not an efficient way to prompt an insight.

The Breaks Can Be More Important Than the Meeting

It's common for meetings to get stuck, and when they do, the most common response is to ignore it and redouble the pressure to have a breakthrough. Instead, as we suggested before, send people on a break when the good feeling is lost. Don't try to recover a lost feeling when under pressure and when thinking is of low quality. Don't fall victim to "just a few minutes more and we can push through." Call a break, and make the break long. Let people go on walks with the assignment to look for fresh thoughts. Or let them simply think about nothing and absorb what they have heard.

Someone will probably come back with an insight that cracks the impasse or problem wide open. Sometimes people with opposing views meet up on their (metaphorical or actual) walks and sort everything out. Even if this doesn't happen, begin the next session by having people report any fresh thoughts they had while on the break, no matter how seemingly inconsequential. Anything fresh can spark an insight on the part of another listener.

For people not familiar with fresh thoughts, or when the group is mixed, Joel has people go on a five-to-ten-minute "sensory walk" by themselves in silence to free up fresh thoughts. Their assignment is to put their entire attention on their senses and notice what they see, hear, smell, and feel. They may become aware of small sounds in the distance or feel the cracks in the sidewalk through their shoes or the hair on their arms being blown by the wind.

They will return with fresh thoughts or a fresh perspective, even if you have not invited them to do so, and the feeling in the room after one of these walks always changes, sometimes quite dramatically.

If You Are the Only One in a Meeting Familiar with The Art of Insight

If you have yet to enroll your team in Insight Thinking, or if you are the only person familiar with this subject, you may face some pretty tough sledding. Even the most well-intentioned people will revert to their habitual styles. Ideally, you should find an internal or external colleague who is skilled at facilitating meetings. A collaboration between two skilled people can usually be quite effective. The simple process is this: You and your facilitator partner should first develop some mastery of The Art of Insight. If you have some honest conversations with each other, you will know when you are ready for "prime time" with your team. Then bring the facilitator in to help run the meeting with you.

Here are a few items for you (or the two of you) to keep in mind:

- *Maintain a good state of mind.* Perhaps the most important point to remember is to maintain your equanimity. By keeping composed and staying conscious of the quality of your state of mind, you will be better equipped to help yourself and others think more effectively. Follow the guidelines for working with a team, even if no one else does. Your equanimity will do a few things:

  - It will make you more able to hear insights of your own that you can then share.
  - It will help you hear and realize the insights of others, which might otherwise be lost in the conversation.
  - It will not contribute to more pressured thinking within the group.
  - In some cases, it might look unusual enough that others will ask what you are doing, which you can then use as an opening to explain Insight Thinking.

- *Use your intuition.* Your instincts are powerful and usually on the mark, so go with your gut if it feels right in the moment.

- *Don't muscle.* These concepts should flow naturally and shouldn't feel like work. If you are trying to "do something" to the room, people will surely notice—and not in a good way.

- *Lead by example.* Illustrate Insight Thinking through your actions and by maintaining a quality state of mind. If you notice that you just interrupted someone to pull her line of thinking toward your own, then you aren't leading very well!

- *Ask high-quality focus questions.* Guide the conversation toward generating good ideas by asking great questions about the subject of the day.

- *Label (out loud) what you are doing when you are doing it.* Say, for example, "Here's a fresh thought," or "I just had a small insight." Like Kay, when you catch yourself about to repeat a memory thought, pause (it's always good to illustrate pausing) and say, "Oh, that's a memory thought someone has already said."

Have faith! Yes, running a meeting like this for the first time is a bit of a leap, so make that first step small. For your part, assume people are capable of generating good insights. If you create the right conditions, a good outcome will occur. You can't "script" the meeting as tightly as perhaps you normally do, so it may feel uncomfortable at first.

If you are the designated meeting leader, consider these thoughts from Jim, one of the in-house facilitators we work with:

> I think you have to feel comfortable knowing that people have the answers within themselves. All the

knowledge the group needs is in the room. The facilitator helps participants look differently at their information and perspectives so they can piece together everything and be confident they can develop effective actions themselves. When group members see they don't really need a lot of external input, that they have all the relevant information, that they just need to give themselves permission to explore and allow the options to bubble up, they're able to recognize their own value, which empowers them.

When I act as facilitator, I also recognize that the way one speaks to a group and settles a room helps people connect with their own innate intelligence. If you absorb the spirit of the room and connect yourself with the undercurrents, you can trust your instincts to come up with something that can unlock the conversation. In my examples, the wisdom of the group surfaced when I followed my own wisdom. If you have an insight or unique way of thinking about the topic under discussion, you may discover a reservoir of strength you can't categorize, but you just go with it.

I might also describe this as the ability to get very, very present. You're not caught up with wondering, "Is this going to work? What are they going to think about me?" You just get really quiet. When you see something that you know is gold, you go with it. You don't have to map it out five blocks or three miles in advance. In the moment, you see what's required,

you know it will work, and you just follow your nose.
I wouldn't say it's a random act, but it's not a staged
operation, either.

Whether you are the leader or the facilitator, you are going
to find using these methods extremely rewarding. Have faith
in your capacity, and remember to maintain a good state of
mind. Those around you will follow your lead, so keep your
composure, trust your instincts, and don't try to force your will
on the room. If you create the right environment, you can have
a creative, efficient meeting every time.

While related, searching for ideas and insights is quite different
from problem solving. Insights can certainly solve problems,
but insights can also illuminate never-before-seen opportunities. Clearly, we want both. Most businesses focus almost exclusively on problem solving at great cost in time and people. In
Western business, we are thoroughly and exclusively trained in
analytic methods, and this is limiting us. It results in ideas and
strategies that are neither insightful nor inspiring to workers.
We could benefit greatly by a complementary focus on insight
generation.

When a person or group has an insight, this has multiple
benefits. Often, these benefits are achieved faster than when the
analytic or problem-solving approach is used. Commitment is
typically high, which leads to rapid implementation. Analysis
can play an essential role in confirming the validity of the

insight, but time and effort are reduced. And of course, insights can often lead to an unusually strong competitive advantage.

The problem-solving route can lead to the selection of the optimal result from an array of known alternatives, but the insight route can lead to something never before conceived. To be sure, without comparing such an insight with the alternatives, there is no assurance that it is the optimal choice, but immediate action on a slightly less-than-optimal path often delivers the better business outcome.

Practicing The Art of Insight is a wonderful experience. It brings out creativity and an innate way of thinking that is both natural and powerful. It positively alters the culture and engagement of organizations and teams. As TAOI is absorbed, people become less stressed. Open space appears on their calendars. Conversations become more relaxed. Relationships improve. People take more initiative and leave work at the end of the day with more energy than when they started.

7 Life in an Insight State

So far, we have focused on creating more in-sights. But you almost certainly have realized by now that the applications and benefits of The Art of Insight reach into every part of our lives.

Based on what we have heard from others, we are confident that as you regain your familiarity with insight and experience a greater number of insights, you will discover positive changes in other areas of your life as well. Thought is at the root of our understanding and our actions. Improved thought leads to improved situations in life more directly than any technique we have come across. If you are relaxed and focused, you make smarter decisions more quickly and with greater confidence than if you are anxious and distracted. You demonstrate better judgment and therefore make fewer mistakes. Your interactions with colleagues improve, and moments of interpersonal conflict disappear. To the calm mind, the world is well paced. Almost miraculously, your personal schedule will relax. You will find plenty of time to live and work with

> To the calm mind,
> the world is
> well paced.

ease. For workplace teams, the effects are multiplied with shorter meetings that flow more efficiently. Better decisions are made, mistakes and errors diminish, and solutions emerge that are easily implemented.

Here is a brief summary of other phenomena that have been consistently reported—benefits for you to look forward to:

You will have lots of little insights and fewer big ones. We believe this is because as you become mindful of small insights, you solve problems earlier—before they grow into bigger issues. Since insights occur all the time, you remain on track, and the need for major epiphanies becomes less frequent.

Life will become easygoing, with fewer problems. Ideas seem to come along just when they're needed. In many cases, these ideas don't register as insights. After a few months, people offer, "I just don't have anything I'd call a real problem."

Your problems will become less emotional and less personal and seem to disappear quickly. You will still get angry or frustrated, but far less frequently and you'll be far more resilient. Issues won't grip you the same way they did before, and you will rid yourself of the bad feeling in a matter of minutes or seconds instead of hours or days.

You will have fewer decisions to make, with less micromanaging. Managers who used to involve themselves in every decision now, curiously, find that team members willingly offer input and recommendations that in most cases are very sound. One client put it well: "The people around me seem to be getting smarter." When controversy arises, managers find themselves leading a discussion and asking questions until there is convergence, as opposed to making tie-breaking decisions.

You will have time for everything. Nearly everyone describes how life feels less pressured and stressed. Fascinating examples include finding less traffic in the morning on the way to work and, most commonly, finding more time. Things don't pile up the way they used to. Meetings end early. Moments of quiet show up throughout the day.

Your communication and relationships will improve. Interpersonal problems diminish. People who have had difficult histories with each other start to get along.

You will gracefully move across all types of thinking. Life is not just about insights. You will routinely move from fresh thinking to memory thinking and from intellect to intuition and enjoy a natural state of flow where you no longer need to consciously decide what type of thinking would work best.

You will have a heightened confidence and a strong sense of peace. Concern, anxiety, and worry become rare. When problems occur, they are just problems, with no ancillary emotionality.

You will find a job you actually love. Usually, this is because people rediscover the ability to enjoy the jobs they have, but in other cases, the perfect job opportunity comes along, and they are alert enough to notice.

You will have more energy. Another client put it nicely, "For the first time in as long as I can remember, I'm bringing all my energy to my life, both at work and at home. I've always felt I had to continually work hard to overcome resistance. Now, it seems like nothing is in my way."

Each person's results are different, of course, and problems will stick. We will still get angry and frustrated when we are in low moods. Everyone loses control once in a while. No one has yet reported any sort of perpetual high, which we think is a good thing. Looking for such a permanent state would probably interfere with finding moments of awe and profound joy. If you notice even a few of the conditions listed above showing up in your life, consider them further evidence of the success of your insight experiment.

Don't Overthink Insight

People who use these methods enjoy a new groove in their lives. Most don't pay a lot of attention to why this is happening or show much interest in being introspective about insight. They say to themselves, "Just be happy and go with the flow." Some of us become more curious about insight and how it occurs, but this isn't necessary and can even carry some risk. It's easy to overthink matters, and studying the Insight State of Mind is no exception. If you become busy-minded about the Insight State of Mind, your experience of that state will almost undoubtedly diminish.

Our client Pete, whom you met before, started learning about insight with a whole raft of problems on his plate. Like many of the people we work with, after a couple of months, all the problems seemed to go away. He still had problems of course, but they weren't major issues. The decisions of his subordinates moved in his favor, often without his conscious attention, and his workplace situation now couldn't look better. Pete doesn't seem to have any particular interest in why this has occurred. He is happy to be, in his words, "hot right now." While he had what must have been an important realization—something about his thinking he didn't understand before—it wasn't of a conceptual nature, and he may never need to articulate it to himself or anybody else. He doesn't even want to. After all, he's "hot"!

An important difference exists between understanding these concepts and having an insight into how you personally think. You want to look for insight into your own thinking process, not just an intellectual understanding of the concept of insight. Once you understand insight as an available tool, once you understand *in your own terms* that insight arrives best from your being in a specific state of mind, and once you understand that this state of mind has a lot to do with the *way you think*, and not so much *what* you think, your life will change. One of the most consistently interesting and important findings of our studies is the value of seeing something for oneself. In the area of Insight Thinking, the benefits come not from having a conceptual understanding but from having an insight into how your own mind works. If you only attain an intellectual mastery of these ideas, you won't have more insights.

At some point, most drivers have experienced a skid starting while making a turn. Your tendency is to steer back onto your course. However, by turning *into* the skid, the car straightens itself, and you stay on the road. In that instant, you may not understand the physics or mechanics of what is happening, but you somehow know what is effective. If you act on that knowing, you will have fewer car wrecks as a result. In the same way, your personal understanding of your capacity for insight can have a profound effect on everything in your life.

Look for That Good Feeling

That's the bottom line. You don't need a conscious change in understanding. The proverbial pennies will drop for you along the way. Perhaps only a few will be in the form of conceptual understandings. All of us walk our own paths to reclaiming our ability for insight. Yours might be a completely nonverbal, even subliminal, experience. You don't need to attach words to it so that you can describe it to yourself, your friends, your families, and colleagues. In fact, your progress in Insight Thinking may be very subtle after a first burst of awareness. Smaller insights may occur with greater frequency, but you may also experience an increase in insights that don't seem to be relevant to anything in the moment. You might be walking to work in the morning and feel hit by an insight of some sort. You know you now understand something you didn't understand before because you have "that" feeling, but your insight doesn't connect to anything you're thinking about at this moment in your life. Only later do a number of these small realizations link together to address something more relevant to you. In some cases, your realizations never link up in a coherent, verbal way. Nevertheless, you wake up one day on a significantly different track in life—a track you know is more authentic for you, one that you have reached with a certain psychological ease.

Reacquainting ourselves with the capacity for insight is something unique, something to be treasured, and that may be the end of it for some of us. If we are asked by others about our process, we might respond that we don't know, but it is common for our friends, families, and coworkers to comment on the changes that they are noticing. Because the experience is not easy to articulate, many of us are content to simply move forward, excited and happy to have a new way of experiencing the world.

Whether or not you have more interest in insight, if you find yourself having more of these experiences and enjoying some of the positive benefits we've discussed, something about insight works for you. It should only get better. We wish you the best in your ongoing explorations.

Assessing Your Progress

As we began our exploration for methods to increase insight and wisdom—what we have come to call The Art of Insight (TAOI) one of our early challenges was that none of our clients had any sense of how often they currently had insights; they only knew that insights didn't come as fre quently as they would like. We wanted to teach our clients some of the ideas we were discovering, but in the absence of a baseline, how could we clearly discern whether someone's "insight meter" had actually changed? At best, our results would be subjective. Our solution was to ask them to make a list of issues, problems, and other situations they wanted insight into, including an assessment of how important each insight was and how long they had struggled with that particular problem. We also asked them to consider what evidence might persuade them that their capacity for insight had increased. Our premise was as follows: if, after a few weeks, our clients either had significant insights on their chosen topics or noticed evidence of an increased capacity for insights, then TAOI would, at least on some level, be proved effective.

If you want to test what you discover about insight, a valuable way to start is by identifying numerous and diverse topics about which you want insights or improved thought. Look for situations, issues, or problems where you currently experience difficulty, opportunities where you want fresh thinking or a new perspective, or simply things you are curious about. Here are some areas to trigger your thinking, along with some examples:

Work: Your relationship with a colleague, boss, or subordinate. A business issue that's remained unsolved for too long. The dynamics of a team of which you are a member.

Family and friends: A difficult relationship. A spot for a vacation everyone would find thrilling. Meeting new friends after a geographical move.

Church/community: Getting the town government to solve a long-standing problem.

Personal: A regular exercise program or other health issue. Finding a new hobby.

A list of between six and ten is good with more than one issue for each heading, but you can have more if you wish. However, don't be concerned if you don't have any issues in a given area, and don't limit yourself to these thought starters. Find what interests you. Don't create another to-do list, attempt to identify *all* the problems in your life, or adopt an action-oriented mind-set. Every issue doesn't need to be serious or consequential. Just develop as broad a range of topics as possible where insights would be helpful to you. For each item, indicate the following:

- How long (days, months, years) has this been an issue?

- On a scale of 1 to 5, how important is it to solve this problem or gain insight into this issue? (1 = a little, 5 = a lot)

A completed item might look like this:

Why does every conversation I have with Jeff seem to meander and never converge? 2+ years, bothers me quite a bit (4).

Return to your list in three or four weeks to finish your experiment. Reflect on each topic and ask yourself, "Have I made any progress on this issue?" Progress might take the form of a partial or complete solution or a drop in the level of importance or bother. Then take an overall look at the list, asking,

- Are all the issues still active?

- Have some issues gone away?

- What happened to the issues that disappeared?

- For those issues still hanging around, have I had any realizations about them? What kind of progress have I made with them?

Online Learning Experience

Visit our website for the Online Learning Experience: www.TAOI-Online-Learning.com.

Notes

Many of the quotes and recollections are from our colleagues and clients. If they aren't referenced below it is because they came from these discussions and interviews.

CHAPTER 1

1. Samuel E. George, letter to the editor, *Wall Street Journal*, August 13, 2008, A16.
2. Eliot Daley, *Formerly Called "Retirement"* (2011), http://www.eliotdaley.com/books/formerly-called-retirement/.
3. *August Rush*, directed by Kirsten Sheridan (Burbank, CA: Warner Bros. Pictures, 2007), film.

CHAPTER 2

1. Bill Russell and Taylor Branch, *Second Wind: The Memoirs of an Opinionated Man* (New York: Random House, 1979).

CHAPTER 3

1. Richard Carlson and Joseph Bailey, *Slowing Down to the Speed of Life: How to Create a More Peaceful, Simpler Life from the Inside Out* (New York: Harper Collins, 1997), 110.

CHAPTER 4

1. T. B. Brazelton and J. K. Nugent, *Neonatal Behavioral Assessment*, 3rd ed. (Cambridge: Cambridge University Press, 1996), cited in *Understanding the Behavior of Term Infants* (March of Dimes, Perinatal Nursing Education, 2003).

CHAPTER 5

1. Graham Wallas, *The Art of Thought* (New York: Harcourt, Brace and Company, 1926).
2. Allison Zmuda, *Breaking Free from Myths about Teaching and Learning: Innovation as an Engine for Student Success* (Alexandria, VA: ASCD, 2010), 181.

CHAPTER 6

1. Robert Fitz, *Creating* (New York: Fawcett Columbine, 1991), 16.

Acknowledgments

A nearly surefire way of elevating your mood is to find someone to whom you are grateful. We could not have written this book without the support of a number of people.

We are especially appreciative of Annika Hurwitt, who first introduced us to some of the key relationships between thought and insight and has contributed enormously to the development of these ideas. Thanks go to George Pransky and his wonderful staff at Pransky & Associates and Roger Mills and the Center for Sustainable Change, all of whom developed and popularized Sydney Banks's seminal insights in this area; Robin Charbit for pioneering with us the direct application of Insight Thinking in business; and Jill Jensen for her work in editing the original essays on which parts of this book are based. Thanks to so many of our clients, associates, and friends, especially Ed Hannifin, Miriam Hawley, Sherry Immediato, Carolyn Kiefer, Megan Kiefer, Ken Manning, Tom McDonough, Doug Milliken, Garret Whitney, Joel Yanowitz, and Allison Zmuda for helping to develop the ideas and contributing their wisdom

Acknowledgments

and wonderful stories, and Steve Tritman for his trenchant criticism as we developed the manuscript.

Special thanks to our family, friends, and loved ones who were steadfast in their support; and finally, we would like to recognize the amazing people at Berrett-Koehler Publishers who have made bringing this book to you an absolute joy.

Index

Index

Index

Index

thinking, *continued*
  good/high-quality, 99–100
  improving your, 107
  insights into nature of your, 106
  overthinking insights, 162–164
  pace of, 42
  reflective, 86–87, 113–114,
    126–127
  relaxation of, 94–95
  state of mind according to style
    of, 163
  techniques for, 59–60
  triggers for assessing your
    progress, 168–169
thought continuum, 40–42
thought/reality relationship, 15, 107
thought(s). *See also* thinking
  allowing wandering, 113, 151–152
  automatic/unconscious switching
    of, 70–71
  conscious, 65
  creation of, 20
  dropping/stopping techniques,
    65–66
  feelings as function of, 99–100
  fresh (*see* fresh thoughts)
  inconsistencies, mistakes, errors,
    inaccuracies in, 115–117
  insights as, 20–24
  insights versus other types of, 19
  listening to your, 63–67
  memory, 20–22, 22–24
  preoccupation with your, 82
  quality of, 57, 95–96
  role of, 103–107
  stopping distracting, 69–79
  thinking pace, 42
  train of, 87
time management, 161
triggers
  for fresh thinking, 168
  of insights, 59, 85
  of low-quality state of mind, 98

of new ideas, 152
for thought derailment, 51

underproductive states, 50–51
understanding
  deepening, through insight, 24–26
  intellectual insight versus, 26
  lack of conscious, 37
  universal, 26
  of yourself, 30–33

vacation state of mind, 103
verification for creative process,
  109, 114
voice types, 90

Wallas, Graham, 109
wandering thoughts, 113, 151–152
wisdom, 56, 80
working alone, 126–127
working with others. *See also*
    conversations; team/group
  applications for TAOI
  clients, 135–137
  facilitating insights in others
    during conversations, 85
  insights into others' behavior,
    28–29
  listening to others, 61–63
  maintaining Insight State of Mind
    when, 127
  practicing with one other person
    (exercises), 67–79
  problem solving for others, 80
  problem solving insights,
    125–126
  working as a trio (exercise and
    examples), 117–125
  writing for insight, 86, 89, 127

Yanowitz, Joel, 131–134

Zmuda, Allison, 123–125

About the Authors

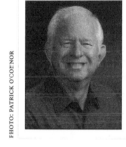

Charles Kiefer

In 1975, Charles Kiefer had an insight that changed the course of his life. Earlier, he had left MIT with degrees in physics and management and had expected to have an exciting career as a management consultant helping high-technology organizations innovate. At the moment of that insight, however, he realized the nature and power of thought and how we create our experience of life. Over the course of the next year, dominoes of insights fell, one of which was the importance and function of vision, both to individuals and to teams and entire organizations. As these insights took hold in his daily life, he became increasingly ill-matched temperamentally to the needs of his employer and was invited to leave.

His first act as a necessity entrepreneur was to start Innovation Associates with a colleague to continue innovation consulting, but every day he was drawn more into improving the quality of people's thinking and specifically employing vision.

Initially, this took the form of developing a program to build high-performing teams. Then, it became apparent that a new vision-based model of leadership was needed. Peter Senge joined him at Innovation Associates, and together they wrote the first published article on the use of vision in organizations. Charlie, Peter, and others at Innovation Associates pressed on, ultimately developing a suite of consulting and training offerings that supported what Peter named a Learning Organization in his management best seller *The Fifth Discipline*. In 1995, they sold the firm to global consulting firm Arthur D. Little.

With vision and organizational learning assumed to be safely in ADL's hands, Charlie turned his attention to insight. When ADL went bankrupt in 2002, he and Robin Charbit formed Charlie's next company, Insight Management Partners, to pioneer the use of insight in large organizations. In 2008, Charlie rekindled a friendship with Len Schlesinger, who had just become president of Babson College, and together they began to explore and develop an understanding of how entrepreneurs think and therefore act. They, with Paul B. Brown, have written two books on this subject: *Action Trumps Everything* and *Just Start*. In 2010, Charlie restarted Innovation Associates as a base for his continued work in insight and entrepreneurial thinking.

He lives with his wife in Sudbury, Massachusetts.

Malcolm Constable

After his junior year at Tufts University, Malcolm Constable spent his summer as an intern at Charlie and Robin's then newly minted Insight Management Partners (a consulting firm helping executives of large corporations access high quality thinking). His compensation was the same insight training that the company was offering its C-suite clients. One sunny afternoon in August, he was participating in a Fresh Thought Hunt around what sort of career he might pursue after college when he had a profound insight that freed him from the narrow way that he had been defining himself. In an instant, a world of opportunities opened in front of him because he no longer viewed his future as being determined by any one decision. This experience allowed him to make a series of life choices that he never would have considered before, but it also made obvious the incredible power of insights. If any question had been left in his mind about whether this "insight stuff" was for real, it was now gone. For the next ten years, regardless of where Malcolm was or what he was doing, his abiding interest in insights helped him stay vigilant about his state of mind, his listening, and particularly his approach to making important decisions.

After graduating from Tufts in 2003 with a degree in English, Malcolm moved to Moscow, where he worked for a consulting firm specializing in oil and gas. After two years in Russia, he returned to Boston to work for Resolve Technology, a commercial real estate consulting firm. In 2007, Charlie floated the idea of Malcolm's returning to Insight Management Partners to work full time. The company was enjoying success helping its clients achieve a significant increase in the frequency and reliability of their strategic insights. Malcolm waited almost two hours before calling back to accept. While working with Charlie, he helped develop a two-day workshop called Insight Golf, which he spun off into a separate company, teaching The Art of Insight to corporate teams using the medium of golf.

Today Malcolm works at a real estate private equity firm, but he still believes deeply in the importance of insights in shaping our world. He lives in Boston and enjoys travel, soccer, golf, and squash.

Berrett–Koehler
Publishers

Berrett-Koehler is an independent publisher dedicated to an ambitious mission: *Creating a World That Works for All.*

We believe that to truly create a better world, action is needed at all levels—individual, organizational, and societal. At the individual level, our publications help people align their lives with their values and with their aspirations for a better world. At the organizational level, our publications promote progressive leadership and management practices, socially responsible approaches to business, and humane and effective organizations. At the societal level, our publications advance social and economic justice, shared prosperity, sustainability, and new solutions to national and global issues.

A major theme of our publications is "Opening Up New Space." Berrett-Koehler titles challenge conventional thinking, introduce new ideas, and foster positive change. Their common quest is changing the underlying beliefs, mindsets, institutions, and structures that keep generating the same cycles of problems, no matter who our leaders are or what improvement programs we adopt.

We strive to practice what we preach—to operate our publishing company in line with the ideas in our books. At the core of our approach is stewardship, which we define as a deep sense of responsibility to administer the company for the benefit of all of our "stakeholder" groups: authors, customers, employees, investors, service providers, and the communities and environment around us.

We are grateful to the thousands of readers, authors, and other friends of the company who consider themselves to be part of the "BK Community." We hope that you, too, will join us in our mission.

A BK Life Book

This book is part of our BK Life series. BK Life books change people's lives. They help individuals improve their lives in ways that are beneficial for the families, organizations, communities, nations, and world in which they live and work. To find out more, visit **www.bk-life.com**.

Berrett–Koehler
Publishers

A community dedicated to creating
a world that works for all

Visit Our Website: www.bkconnection.com

Read book excerpts, see author videos and Internet movies, read
our authors' blogs, join discussion groups, download book apps, find
out about the BK Affiliate Network, browse subject-area libraries of
books, get special discounts, and more!

Subscribe to Our Free E-Newsletter, the *BK Communiqué*

Be the first to hear about new publications, special discount offers,
exclusive articles, news about bestsellers, and more! Get on the list
for our free e-newsletter by going to **www.bkconnection.com**.

Get Quantity Discounts

Berrett-Koehler books are available at quantity discounts for orders
of ten or more copies. Please call us toll-free at (800) 929-2929 or
email us at bkp.orders@aidcvt.com.

Join the BK Community

BKcommunity.com is a virtual meeting place where people from
around the world can engage with kindred spirits to create a world
that works for all. BKcommunity.com members may create their own
profiles, blog, start and participate in forums and discussion groups,
post photos and videos, answer surveys, announce and register for
upcoming events, and chat with others online in real time. Please join
the conversation!